OIL AND GAS PRODUCTION

*An Introductory Guide to Production Techniques
and Conservation Methods*

OIL AND GAS PRODUCTION

An Introductory Guide

to PRODUCTION TECHNIQUES *and*

CONSERVATION METHODS

COMPILED BY THE
ENGINEERING COMMITTEE
INTERSTATE OIL COMPACT COMMISSION

PUBLISHED FOR THE
INTERSTATE OIL COMPACT COMMISSION
BY THE
UNIVERSITY OF OKLAHOMA PRESS
NORMAN

COPYRIGHT 1951 BY THE UNIVERSITY OF OKLAHOMA PRESS
PUBLISHING DIVISION OF THE UNIVERSITY
COMPOSED AND PRINTED AT NORMAN, OKLAHOMA, U.S.A.
BY THE UNIVERSITY OF OKLAHOMA PRESS
FIRST EDITION, JUNE, 1951
SECOND PRINTING, JULY, 1951

THE ENGINEERING COMMITTEE
INTERSTATE OIL COMPACT COMMISSION

W. H. Carson (chairman), Norman, Oklahoma

Eugene A. Stephenson, Lawrence, Kansas

F. M. Van Tuyl, Golden, Colorado

William J. Murray, Jr., Austin, Texas

R. L. Kenan, Montgomery, Alabama

Jack Sanders, El Dorado, Arkansas

Joseph Weil, Gainesville, Florida

A. G. Stanford, Atlanta, Georgia

Ivan G. Burrell, Terre Haute, Indiana

Ralph Esarey, Bloomington, Indiana

Richard Haskell, New York, New York

Tom M. Winfiele, Baton Rouge, Louisiana

Lee S. Miller, Lansing, Michigan

H. M. Morse, Jackson, Mississippi

John Bukvich, Butte, Montana

R. R. Spurrier, Santa Fé, New Mexico

G. W. Holbrook, Wellsville, New York

E. V. O'Rourke, Columbus, Ohio

A. W. Gauger, State College, Pennsylvania

Paul Price, Morgantown, West Virginia

G. W. Govier (associate member), Edmonton,
Alberta, Canada

FOREWORD

This book is sponsored by the Interstate Oil Compact Commission, an association of twenty sovereign oil and gas producing states which have executed the Interstate Compact to Conserve Oil and Gas, to which the Congress of the United States has given its approval.

The Compact Commission is composed of the governors, and their representatives, of oil and gas producing states and operates in the public interest in an effort to promote better oil and gas conservation programs.

As set out in Article II of the Interstate Compact: "The purpose of this Compact is to conserve oil and gas by the prevention of physical waste thereof from any cause."

As defined in Article VI: "The duty of the Compact Commission is to make inquiry and ascertain from time to time such methods, practices, circumstances, and conditions as may be disclosed for bringing about conservation and the prevention of physical waste of oil and gas, and at such intervals as said Commission deems beneficial it shall report its findings and recommendations to the several states for adoption or rejection."

The Interstate Oil Compact Commission recommends this volume, prepared by its Engineering Committee, as an instrument for promotion of better oil and gas conservation and in line with the purposes of the Compact.

EARL FOSTER
Executive Secretary

Interstate Oil Compact Commission
P.O. Box 3127, State Capitol
Oklahoma City, Oklahoma

INTRODUCTION

Oil and gas conservation in its broadest sense means the use of the most efficient methods of discovery, development, and production to insure the greatest recovery of oil and gas from nature's reservoirs.

The Interstate Oil Compact Commission, which, at the time of the writing of this volume comprises twenty oil-producing states, was formed in 1935 for the purpose of conserving oil and gas by the prevention of physical waste thereof from any cause. Being without executive or administrative power, the Compact Commission has sought to further conservation through educational efforts. Its member states, through their administrative officials and technical staffs, have collected and co-ordinated information about the technical advances being made in the production and conservation of oil and gas, and the Compact Commission, through its *Quarterly Bulletin* and other publications, has kept its member states and the public informed of these engineering advances.

It is the purpose of this volume to offer, in convenient form, to all interested in the efficient recovery of oil and gas, a practical treatise covering present knowledge on the occurrence of oil and gas, the nature of the reservoirs in which they are found, and the technical science of utilizing and supplementing in the most efficient manner the natural forces available in the reservoir for the greatest recovery of oil and gas for public use. This book, then, represents the co-ordination by the Compact's Engineering Committee of the knowledge of administrative and technical men on the staffs of the various states, the educational institutions of those states, and engineers, geologists, chemists, and technical men of the oil and gas industry.

The editors have endeavored to treat all subjects in a practical and understandable manner, as free as possible from technical terms. The behavior of an oil or gas reservoir as production takes place is as unpredictable as a human being's reaction to changes in environment unless the separate and distinct characteristics which govern its reactions are known. In this publication general statements are made to minimize detail and confusion; therefore, modification is necessary in their application to the specific problems of any one oil or gas reservoir. It is hoped that through these pages the oil producers, royalty owners, lawyers, legislators, and laymen may be aided in learning the principles of efficient oil and gas reservoir control. When properly observed, the practices described will make available for public use the greatest possible amount of these nonreplaceable natural resources.

All of the illustrations which carry the credit, "After LeRoy" or "Modified after LeRoy," are used with the permission of Professor Leslie W. LeRoy and the Colorado School of Mines.

This publication is the result of untiring effort on the part of many persons, and the Editorial Subcommittee of the Engineering Committee wishes to thank them warmly for their contributions.

Editorial Subcommittee
EUGENE A. STEPHENSON
F. M. VAN TUYL
W. H. CARSON

March 17, 1951

CONTENTS

FIGURES

TABLES

OIL AND GAS PRODUCTION

An Introductory Guide to Production Techniques
and Conservation Methods

CHAPTER I

PETROLEUM GEOLOGY

Introduction

The user of liquid fuel in a late-model, streamlined automobile is rarely aware that he is a participant in the final act of a fascinating drama whose scenes span a period of several hundred million years. Nevertheless, such is the case when gasoline is burned in the engines of motor vehicles. The consumption of lubricants, kerosene, diesel fuel, and other petroleum products marks the end of this drama.

Attempts to decipher the events of the remote geological past are based on the fact that evidence of all active geologic processes of the past can be observed in operation at the present. Familiarity with the operation of such processes as they function today makes it possible to reconstruct the scenes of geologic history when the essential field and laboratory information has been obtained and organized. Where insufficient data are available, tentative working hypotheses are of great value. They may stimulate the search for new data whose importance had hitherto been unsuspected. Such hypotheses may be modified or discarded as additional information is forthcoming, until overwhelming evidence points finally to the correct conclusion or interpretation.

Historical Geology

Historical geology endeavors to trace the successive events in the physical history of the earth, the origin and evolution of life, the distribution of lands and seas during the various geologic periods, and the development of the rocks of different ages.

The age of the earth is almost incomprehensible. It is estimated to be more than two billion years. The major changes that affect the surface of the earth have been, and continue to be, scarcely perceptible during the lifetime of an individual. However, given sufficient time, "nothing is more changeable than the everlasting hills." The mountains of today are of relatively recent age, geologically speaking. Many of them occur in areas that have been repeatedly occupied by the sea. In many instances ancient sediments left by the sea carry fossil remains of marine life. After the mountains are worn away through the slow processes of erosion and the transportation of waste material to lower areas, including the ocean, the sea may return to submerge extensive areas of land. Later, portions of the eroded lands again may be raised into mountains or highlands. The newly created landscapes in turn yield to the same erosional and deformational processes. Over a period of hundreds of millions of years the cycle of land destruction, submergence, deposition, and elevation may be repeated over and over again with greater or less intensity.

These same cycles have rarely, if ever, occurred simultaneously at all points on the surface of the continents. Submergence may take place in one area at the same time as uplift and erosion in another. Rocks formed during one period may be uplifted and at least partially eroded to form the debris deposited in the sea or elsewhere on the land. If the sediments are deposited upon an eroded surface, they are said to be *unconformable* with the rocks below.

Unconformities (Figure 1) indicate the location and time at which profound changes in the physical history of an area have taken place. They indicate also the geographic positions of land and sea in ancient times and provide a basis for separation of rocks into their various ages. In terms of the analogy of the drama, the unconformities represent the changes in scenes and acts or the periods between the scenes and acts.

The present distribution and character of sedimentary deposits, taking into consideration loss by erosion, make it possible to represent on maps the position of the ancient seas and their shore lines, the regions of continental deposition, and the location and relative elevation of lands supplying sediments. The extent and position of the lands and seas change from period to period (Figures 2a and 2b). Where the data are reasonably complete, such maps are of considerable value. They indicate the

4

Fig. 1.—Unconformity, showing nearly vertical beds below,
overlain by gently dipping strata.

location of near-shore or shallow-water deposits which are more
prolific sources of petroleum and gas than the more open-sea
types. Furthermore, discontinuous porous sandstones and limestones capable of serving as traps for oil and gas are more common in these areas.

If it were possible to turn the sedimentary layers backward
as leaves in a book, it would be found that the contents of this
great book may be divided into chapters related to life on and a
description of the nature of the earth as it existed over a span of
many millions of years. Geologically speaking, these chapter-
time intervals are referred to as *eras*. The geologic time scale
(Table I) presents the commonly recognized names for the various eras and smaller divisions of geologic time as well as the rocks
of the geologic column formed during these intervals of time.

During each era severe readjustments within the earth made
many changes in the structure of the earth's crust (the outer por-

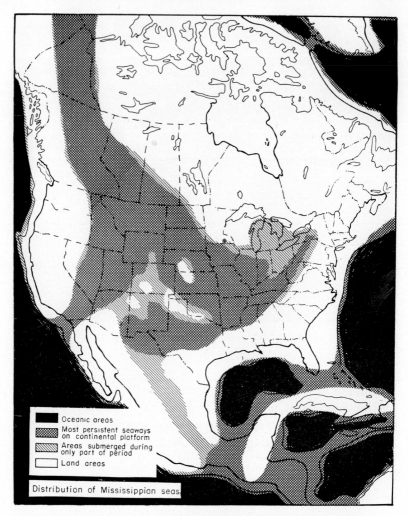

Fig. 2a.—Present-day map of North America superimposed on map of North America during Mississippian geologic period. From *Introduction to Historical Geology*, by R. C. Moore (copyright 1949). Courtesy McGraw-Hill Book Company.

tion of the earth, which may be a number of miles in thickness). These structural changes took place in various *periods* of an era. During the millions of years in a period, the changes on the earth's surface were of varying intensity. Sediments that were deposited

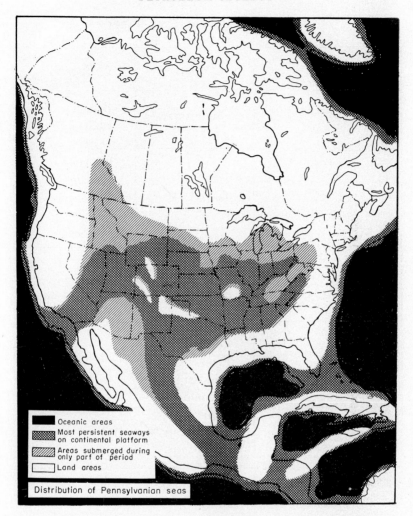

Oceanic areas
Most persistent seaways on continental platform
Areas submerged during only part of period
Land areas

Distribution of Pennsylvanian seas

Fig. 2b.—Present-day map of North America superimposed on map of North America during Pennsylvanian geologic period. From *Introduction to Historical Geology*, by R. C. Moore (copyright 1949). Courtesy McGraw-Hill Book Company.

during the more recent periods have certain identifiable colors, texture, and remains of plant and animal life that make possible a further division called *epochs*.

7

TABLE I. GEOLOGIC TIME TABLE

Era	Period	Epoch
Cenozoic	Quaternary	Recent Pleistocene
	Tertiary ✓	Pliocene Miocene Oligocene Eocene Paleocene
Mesozoic	Cretaceous ✓ Jurassic Triassic	
Paleozoic	Permian ✓ Pennsylvanian ✓ Mississippian ✓ Devonian ✓ Silurian Ordovician ✓ Cambrian	
Proterozoic	Pre-Cambrian	Keweenawan Huronian
Archeozoic (Oldest)	Pre-Cambrian	Timiskamian Keewatin

Oil formations have been named according to local customs. For example, one oil formation of Ordovician age in Oklahoma is called the Wilcox sandstone. An oil formation of Cretaceous age in Texas is known as the Woodbine sand. An oil formation of Devonian age in New York is the Richburg sand.

Many gaps or lost intervals appear in the record, some of which involve millions of years. They indicate times of erosion on the continents and are represented by unconformities. Geologic history, like human history, has many imperfections in the record.

Fossils (the remains of animals or plants, or their impressions, preserved in the sedimentary rocks) are the chief source of information regarding the origin and evolution of life. They indicate the ages as well as the environmental conditions that prevailed during the deposition of the sediments that contain them. For this reason, historical geology is based largely upon the study of the sedimentary formations.

Commercial accumulations of petroleum occur in rocks of almost every known era, although they are not uniformly distributed throughout the geologic column. The most productive systems the world over, from the standpoint of oil yield to date, are Tertiary, Cretaceous, Permian, Pennsylvanian, Mississippian, Devonian, and Ordovician.

Structural Geology

Most sedimentary deposits were formed through the accumulation of eroded material in seas, lakes, and streams. Other deposits were formed by chemical precipitation of material from solution and by the accumulation of organic remains. They were laid down in nearly horizontal layers; yet old formations of this type are found today tilted at all angles. Sedimentary rocks may be exposed and observed in hillside cliffs (Figure 3), mountains, quarries, and highway cuts. Tilting apparently plays an important role in the development of oil and gas reservoirs. Commercial accumulations of oil and gas are found in strata which are folded, or at least tilted in some degree. The heaviest deposition of sediments was in large basins or depressions of vast extent where downward settling occurred as a result of overloading with debris from near-by lands. Thousands of feet of sedimentary rocks may accumulate over areas varying in size from less than one thousand square miles to tens of thousands of square miles. The deposits become thinner around the edges of the basins. Most of the important oil-producing regions of the world are in basins of sedimentation of this type.

The shift of countless tons of material from land to sea and from highland to lowland on the continents through the perpetual processes of erosion, transportation, and sedimentation, as well as other readjustments, set up strains at different places in the rocks of the outer portion of the earth. These strains were so great that they were eventually relieved by the mass movement and deformation of the rocks as they became adjusted to the new conditions. Broad regional uplifts or downward settling took place along with local gentle folding and minor faulting (displacement along fractures, Figure 4) of sedimentary strata that

Fig. 3.—Outcrop of sedimentary rock, showing layers and stratification.

originally were laid down in approximately horizontal layers. In other localities the sedimentary rocks are more extensively folded and faulted (Figure 5). The over-all result of folding and tilting has been the development of geologic structures called *anticlines* (Figure 6), *synclines* (Figure 7), *domes* (Figure 6), and *monoclines* (Figure 8), which are of great importance in localizing accumulations of petroleum and natural gas.

Unequal erosion of upturned strata of variable resistance may result in the development of rim rocks or hogback ridges of hard

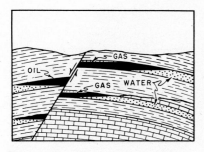

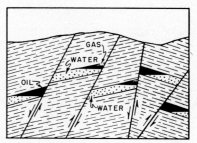

Fig. 4.—Cross section showing displacement of rock layers along a fracture. Oil and gas traps may occur on both sides of the fault. (After LeRoy)

Fig. 5.—Numerous faults with oil traps in each fault block. The faults may extend horizontally for miles. (After LeRoy)

beds. The nature, extent, and steepness of the folds may be disclosed by these features. Several types of oil and gas traps may exist both below and above an unconformity (Figures 9 and 10). Renewed deformation in such areas may increase the dips of the earlier folds and develop gentle dip structures in the sediments which blanket the area.

Extensive forest covering, thick mantles of gravel, sand, or soil, glacial debris, or large bodies of water may conceal the bedrock and make it impossible to find exposures (outcrops) by which subsurface structures may be located.

Reservoir Rocks

The various types of rocks that comprise the outer portion of the earth are classified as igneous, metamorphic, and sedimen-

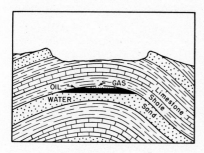

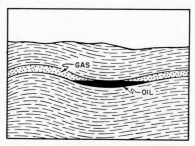

Fig. 6.—Anticline or dome with trap for oil and gas. Anticlines are elongated domes.

Fig. 7.—A syncline with oil and gas trap.

11

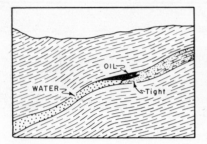

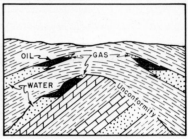

Fig. 8.—A monocline. The upper boundary of the oil trap is tight rock. (After LeRoy)

Fig. 9.—Oil traps above and below an unconformity and buried ridge.

tary. Only sedimentary rocks are of major importance in petroleum geology.

The most common types of reservoir rocks are the coarser sedimentary rocks such as *sands, sandstones,* and *conglomerates.* Sands and sandstones are composed almost entirely of quartz grains. Impure sands contain clay or silt particles which tend to clog the openings between the grains. Rocks of the older geologic series are well consolidated, while those of more recent epochs are little consolidated. Relatively young sands and sandstones are more porous and permeable than the older types which have been more deeply buried, compacted, and cemented. Based upon the predominant types of cementing material present, most sandstones may be classified as *calcareous, dolomitic, siliceous,* or *ferruginous.* Conglomerates (consolidated gravels) are composed

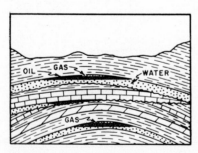

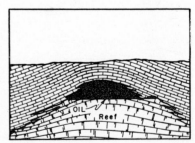

Fig. 10.—Another example of oil traps above and below an unconformity. (After LeRoy)

Fig. 11.—Limestone reef trap.

12

of pebbles of various sizes held together by the same type of cementing materials as sandstone.

Many reservoirs occur in the *Carbonate rocks, limestone,* and *dolomite.* Many forms of marine life extract the lime from sea water and use it in building their shells or body structures. After death the organic matter decays and the calcareous skeletal material accumulates to form the limestone. Limestones also form as chemical precipitates when soluble bicarbonate of lime loses carbon dioxide. Porous reef limestone masses were built in a marine environment. Muds and other types of fine-grain sediments flank and overlie the porous reef mass to form traps for prolific petroleum reservoirs (Figure 11).

Limestones made up of rounded grains, resembling in form and size the eggs of fish, are termed *oolitic.* They resemble ordi-

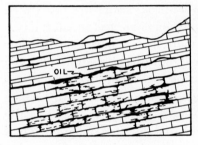

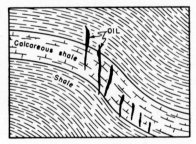

Fig. 12.—Oil in crevices and solution cavities of limestone.

Fig. 13.—Oil in shale crevices.

nary sands in their behavior as reservoir rocks. Many highly productive petroleum reservoirs are found in fractured limestones and dolomites with more or less well-developed solution cavities and perhaps other types of openings (Figure 12).

Of the various kinds of sedimentary rocks, *shales* predominate, constituting approximately 80 per cent of the total. Shales are finely divided particles of older rocks (compacted muds) which were deposited in the still waters of seas and lakes. Many shale beds contain finely disseminated organic residues. They are believed to have constituted the most important source beds for petroleum and natural gas.

13

Shales are highly compacted sediments that can serve as reservoirs for oil and gas only under exceptional circumstances, as where fissures and fractures are present (Figure 13). Such fractures and crevices containing oil or gas may occur in close association with shale source beds or with pools of oil and gas in sandstone or limestone reservoirs. They appear to function in part as connecting drainage channels. A number of sensational but short-lived wells and a few low-capacity, long and steady producers have been completed in fractured shales.

Salt, gypsum, and *anhydrite* are of little importance as reservoirs. Evaporation causes supersaturation of saline water and results in the chemical precipitation of the salts to form these rocks which tend to yield under pressure. At substantial depths below the surface their capacity to hold fluids has been greatly reduced by compaction.

A few instances are known where coal seams are penetrated by wells that produce up to two million cubic feet of gas a day.

All sedimentary rocks were more or less porous at the time of their deposition. Later they may have been modified through compaction, cementation, fracturing, solution, and other processes. Gravels have become conglomerates, sands have become sandstones, and muds and clays have changed to shales, while many limestones have been altered to dolomites. Where original sediments have been poorly sorted, all gradations may occur between conglomerates and sandstones, sandstones and shales, sandstones and limestones, and shales and limestones.

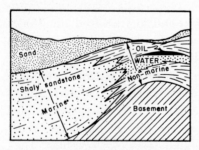

Fig. 14.—Gradation from sand to shale in rocks deposited near the shore of an ancient sea. (After LeRoy)

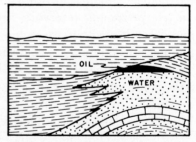

Fig. 15.—Gradation from shale to sand. (After LeRoy)

14

Individual formations range in thickness from a few inches to more than one thousand feet. They may gradually change laterally, wholly or in part, from one kind to another within relatively short distances. This is known as a *change in facies.* Thus, a shale may grade shoreward into a sand or sandstone (Figures 14 and 15).

Oil, gas, and petroleum residues, such as asphalt, have been found in igneous and metamorphic rocks in a few places, but their commercial importance is very limited.

Origin and Accumulation of Hydrocarbons

A generally accepted and wholly adequate theory concerning the origin and accumulation of petroleum has not yet been devised. It is commonly believed that low forms of both plant and animal life provided the primary source material for the hydrocarbons. Subsequent putrefaction of the organic matter in conjunction with bacterial action may have eliminated the constituents other than fats, oily substances, and related materials. Through modifications not yet fully understood, these substances were changed to gaseous and liquid hydrocarbons. Much laboratory and field work supports these views. Compaction of sediments, especially muds, causing a marked reduction in pore space, may represent an important cause of movement of water and hydrocarbons upward and outward into porous rocks known as *reservoir horizons.* Those portions of the porous zone which carry concentrations of oil and gas are called the *reservoirs,* while this zone throughout its extent is referred to as the *reservoir horizon.* Final concentration of petroleum in the reservoir itself evidently occurred as a result of buoyancy, the propulsive force of moving gas, and the circulation of underground water. For the most part, the time during which commercial accumulation of oil took place has followed rather than preceded the folding or tilting of the strata.

Oil and gas occur underground as concentrations in:

1. porous and permeable rocks such as sands and sandstones with small open spaces between the grains (intergranular spaces) and in limestones and dolomites with a variety of

15

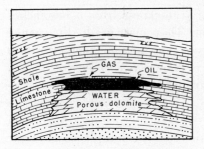

Fig. 16.—Oil and gas trap in porous, permeable stratum. Reservoir sealed on top by impervious shale bed, on bottom by water-saturated zone. Tight limestone flanks the reservoir trap.

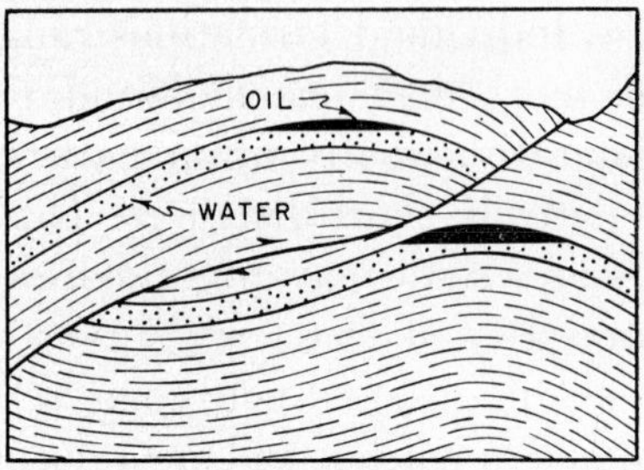

Fig. 17.—Reservoirs in folded and faulted strata. Water underlies the oil. (After LeRoy)

openings such as small spaces between oolites or other grains;

2. open joints, fractures, and bedding planes;
3. small, irregular, and often discontinuous solution cavities not directly related to other structures;
4. buried caves, sometimes connected by channels, produced by the solution action of ground waters moving along bedding planes, joints, and other types of fractures; and
5. a combination of two or more of the above types.

Because porous rocks absorb water more readily than oil and because some of the pores are minute in size, a film of water is usually found on the surface of the mineral grains. This water, which is normally saline, is the residue from buried sea water that was incompletely displaced by oil and gas at the time they accumulated. The concept that most oil exists as underground pools or lakes is devoid of factual basis.

The geological features necessary to the accumulation of oil and gas in commercial reservoirs are:

1. a porous, permeable zone of sufficient thickness to contain large quantities of oil and gas;
2. an overlying impervious bed;
3. an underlying seal, such as a water-saturated zone or a pinch-out of the oil-bearing stratum (Figure 16); and
4. some type of structural feature, or a discontinuity of the

16

porous, permeable beds, or a combination of the two that provided a trap in which the petroleum or natural gas accumulated and was preserved.

The periods of both origin and accumulation may be thought of as scenes in the drama of petroleum with the shifting sea and land as "props" or settings for the performance. The actors were those myriad forms of marine life which lived for a brief moment of geological history, then quickly passed to death and entombment or perhaps were completely obliterated.

Reservoirs are normally confined by water downdip below the oil or gas in the reservoir horizon (Figure 17). The other boundaries may be the result of such features as closure in the

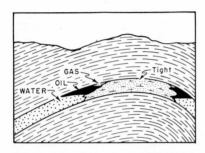

Fig. 18.—Boundary of reservoir updip is tight rock formed either by cementation or by lateral gradation. (After LeRoy)

trap (Figure 19), cementation of the reservoir-rock updip (Figure 18), lateral gradation of the reservoir into shale or other impervious rock (Figure 16), faulting of impervious strata against the reservoir (Figure 5), or a combination of two or more of these or other relationships.

The vertical extent of the reservoir horizon, measured above the point where the direction of dip or slope is changed in magnitude, is commonly called the *structural relief* or *closure,* even though all of that part above the point of reversal or change in dip may not be saturated with petroleum (Figure 19). The amount of relief encountered ranges from a few feet to several thousand feet.

17

A discussion of the major types of reservoir traps may be found in the appendix.

Oil Finding

The selection of areas favorable for the occurrence of oil and gas is a complex problem which should be carefully considered before test (wildcat) wells are drilled. Reconnaissance surveys involve gathering preliminary information on seepages and other direct evidences of petroleum or natural gas, location and extent of sufficient outcrops to justify detailed mapping, study of regional and local structure, study of thickness and character of sedimentary formations with particular attention to potential source beds and reservoir horizons, determination of the presence

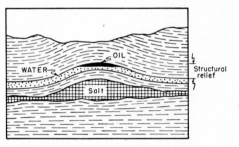

Fig. 19.—Non-piercement salt dome. Structural relief or closure of reservoir horizon is shown. (Modified after LeRoy)

or absence of unconformities in the section, the possibility of the existence of traps other than anticlines and domes, and any other pertinent information. Aerial photographs, topographic maps, and base maps that show roads and trails may be very helpful in early surveys. Should the preliminary studies indicate encouraging results, they are followed up by detailed surveys with the alidade and plane table or other standard methods in order to locate the most favorable places for drilling operations.

In many instances the folded rocks are hidden by deposits of more or less horizontal character, and the surface beds afford little or no clue to the underground structure. A thorough knowledge of the geologic history of the region and of structural habits and trends becomes useful in the search for hidden or subsurface structures.

Various types of maps, models, block diagrams, and cross sections are employed to show the geologic structures and other features designated as traps wherein oil may have accumulated. The most common method for the representation of geologic structure is the *structure contour map* (Figure 20). On such a map the attitude of any particular bed or stratum, known as a *key bed*, is represented by structure contour lines that connect points of

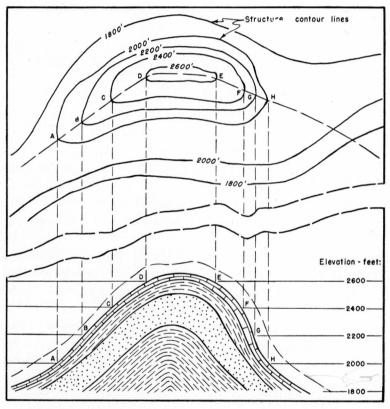

Fig. 20.—Subsurface contour map (above) of anticline shown in cross section (below). The area within the 2,000-foot contour constitutes the closed area.

equal elevation on the top or the base of the bed. The *contour interval* is the vertical distance between adjacent lines or contours. It ranges from as little as one foot for structures of low relief to more than one hundred feet for structures of great relief.

The contour map may indicate the structure of the underlying rocks and the presence of a trap. Use is made of records of the various wells that have been drilled in the general area, even though such wells have been unproductive. Electrical logs of the wells, the cores that have been taken during drilling, the cuttings from completed wells (whether dry or productive), and the fossil content, as well as the mineralogical features of the cores and cuttings, all help to make clearer the picture of the underground formations.

Minute fossils, such as Foraminifera, have been found widely distributed throughout the geologic column. Some of these characterize a particular geologic stratum, and the bed may even be named for its unique fossils. Other rocks, notably the dolomites, have insoluble or siliceous residues that are peculiar to a particular formation throughout a wide area, and thus assist in identification of strata which otherwise cannot be correlated.

The information secured from the first well drilled in a new area shows the sequence of beds penetrated, although it reveals little about the subsurface structure. As other wells are completed, data are acquired that make possible the construction of a subsurface contour map. The accuracy of maps so constructed increases with each new well completed, until finally the entire structure is portrayed and the boundaries of the field established.

A further contribution to oil finding has been made by use of geophysical methods where surface exposures are absent or inadequate to reveal the geologic structure. The *gravity meter* has been particularly useful in the location of salt domes, since the salt mass has a lower average density or specific gravity than other rock masses and its gravitational attraction is less. The *magnetometer*, which measures the relative intensity of the earth's magnetic effect, is of special value where salt or igneous or metamorphic rocks are more or less responsible for the real or apparent structure. The *seismograph* is used to measure either refracted or reflected artificial waves induced through the detonation of high explosives. Seismic studies have proved especially satisfactory where the sediments consist of alternating layers of different thickness and character. Structural features to depths of more than 15,000 feet have been discovered by these means. Reflection shooting is now the method most commonly used. A few studies in earth resistivity have been carried on and are still in progress. The method has proved rather successful in the detection of metallic minerals. The need is great for new geophysical techniques that will supplement those already in use.

Serious attempts have been made over a period of years to utilize precise soil analyses (geochemical prospecting) for the detection of traces of the lighter hydrocarbons and the location of special concentrations which may indicate possible oil and gas reservoirs. Even though incredibly minute quantities of hydrocarbons can be accurately detected, the results have not been as promising as had been hoped.

CHAPTER II

RESERVOIR FLUIDS

Distribution of Fluids Within the Reservoir

During the period of accumulation of petroleum and natural gas in the reservoir trap, some of the buried sea water was displaced. In the course of time, gravitational forces separated the mixture of gas, petroleum, and the remaining water into layers (Figure 21). This arrangement is somewhat similar to the separation that can be seen when a mixture of oil, water, and gas is placed in a glass bottle and allowed to stand for a short time. Gravitational forces will cause the gas to rise to the top and the water to settle to the bottom, the oil forming a layer between the gas and the water. In the bottle, a sharp line of demarcation can be noted between the three layers. In the reservoir, however, the line of demarcation is not so clearly defined because of the effect of capillary forces. Capillary forces are those which enable the fine-pore spaces in a lamp wick to hold kerosene above the liquid level in the lamp well. In the same way, capillary forces enable the fine-pore spaces of the granular reservoir rock to hold some of the water above the water layer.

The gas layer is called the *gas-cap*, the petroleum layer is called the *oil zone*, and the water layer, the *water zone*. The line of demarcation between the gas-cap and the oil zone is the gas-oil contact, and the line between the water zone and the oil zone is the water-oil contact. The relative amounts of oil, gas, and water within a given portion of the reservoir are denoted by the term *saturation*. For example, a reservoir is 30 per cent saturated with oil if that liquid occupies 30 per cent of the total pore space.

Reservoir Water

The water present throughout the zones occupied by the natural gas and oil is called *interstitial*, or *connate*, water. The finer

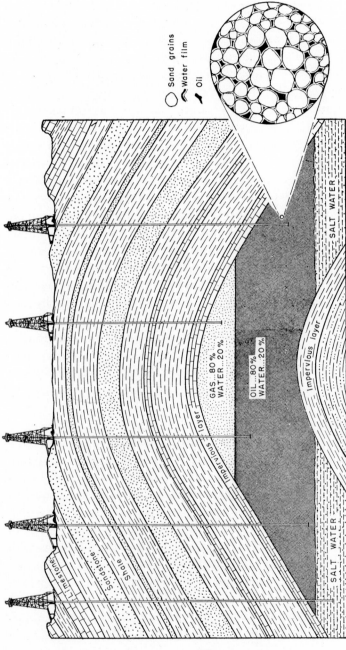

Fig. 21.—Distribution of fluids within a reservoir. At right is a magnified view of sand grains, with film of water around each grain and oil in remainder of pore space.

23

the pore channels between the mineral grains of the rock, the larger the percentage of pore space that will be filled with water throughout the oil and gas zones. Where clay or adsorptive minerals are present, comparatively large quantities of water are found. Very little, if any, of the water held by capillary forces throughout the reservoir is produced into the wells.

Reservoir water may be fresh, brackish, or saline, but is usually saline. The total salinity may reach approximately 25 per cent by weight of solids, or about seven times that of sea water. The greatest portion of these solids is salt (sodium chloride), but lesser amounts of other chlorides, carbonates, and sulfates are also present. A few instances have been reported in which salt comprises slightly more than 99 per cent of the total solids in the water. In general the chemical nature of the solids depends upon the make-up of the ancient sea within which the sediments were deposited and upon later geological changes. The salinity may have been reduced through dilution with fresh water, concentrated by evaporation of the water, or altered chemically by bacterial action.

Although water is but slightly compressible, nevertheless, at the high pressures in many of the deep reservoirs this compressibility provides an important source of energy for the production of oil and gas.

Petroleum and Natural Gas

Petroleum is a general term that is commonly applied to the combustible liquids withdrawn from the earth. It is made up of a mixture of an enormous number of individual organic compounds composed of hydrogen and carbon, which are known as hydrocarbons. Impurities, such as carbon dioxide, nitrogen, helium, and compounds of sulfur and oxygen, are sometimes associated with petroleum. Helium in gases is usually associated with nitrogen. Sulfur, even in small amounts, imparts a foul odor and induces a corrosive character to oil and gas, which fluids are called *sour*.

The three types of crude petroleum are designated as *paraffin base, asphaltic base,* and *mixed base.* These terms denote

24

the chemical nature of the chief hydrocarbon constituents of a crude. Paraffin-base oils are usually lighter in color and gravity than the asphaltic oils and are excellent sources of high-grade lubricants. Asphaltic-base oils are superior sources of motor fuels.

The most important physical properties of crude petroleum are *specific gravity* (comparative weight) and *viscosity* (fluidity). These determine to a large extent the behavior of the fluid within the reservoir. Another important physical property, *the cloud point,* is the temperature at which solid hydrocarbons form and at which the viscosity increases markedly. Fundamentally, all of these properties are dependent upon the kind and abundance of the various hydrocarbons present. The solid hydrocarbons are *bitumen, asphalt,* and *paraffin.* They may be deposited within the reservoir rock, well equipment, or surface lines and tanks. Occasionally they are found as natural deposits, so intimately mixed with mineral grains that they can be used as road-surface material with little or no special treatment.

The simplest hydrocarbons associated with petroleum are *methane, ethane, propane,* and *butane,* which are gaseous at ordinary atmospheric conditions. Of these, methane is the lightest and most abundant, with ethane next. Propane and butane have slightly more complex molecular structures, and, though present in gaseous form, are readily converted to the liquid state. Still greater complexity of molecular structure characterizes the next members of the paraffin series, *pentane, hexane, heptane,* and *octane,* all of which are liquid at ordinary atmospheric conditions, although small amounts of each may be present in the gas associated with petroleum. The quantity in the gaseous state decreases with increase in molecular weight.

While each of the compounds from butane through octane (see Table II) has its distinct and fixed chemical composition, it may have more than one type of molecular structure. Compounds that have the same composition but differ in the arrangement of the atoms within the molecule are known as *isomers.* As a result of the many possible positions of the carbon and hydrogen atoms with respect to each other in the molecule, the heavier hydrocarbons consist of almost unlimited numbers of compounds that

TABLE II

PHYSICAL PROPERTIES OF A FEW OF THE NATURAL HYDROCARBONS

Name	Chemical Formula	Condition at 60° F. and 14.65 psia	Molecular Weight	Density Gas*	Density Liquid†	Boiling Point F.°, at Normal Condition	Critical Temp. F.°	Critical Temp. Absolute°	Critical Pressure psia	Weight of Liquid Lbs. Per Gallon	Heating Value: B.T.U. per Pound
Methane	CH_4	Gas	16.04	0.559	----	-258.5	-116	344	673	----	23,571
Ethane	C_2H_6	"	30.07	1.037	----	-127.5	89	549	712	----	21,876
Propane	C_3H_8	"	44.09	1.521	0.510	- 43.9	205	666	617	4.25	21,646
N-Butane	C_4H_{10}	"	58.12	2.004	0.584	31.1	306	766	551	4.86	21,293
iso-Butane	C_4H_{10}	"	58.12	2.004	0.564	13.6	272	732	544	4.69	21,242
N-Pentane	C_5H_{12}	Liquid	72.15	2.491	0.6304	96.9	386	846	485	5.25	20,914
iso-Pentane	C_5H_{12}	"	72.15	2.494	0.6241	82.3	370	829	483	5.20	20,877
N-Hexane	C_6H_{14}	"	86.17	2.975	0.6634	155.8	454	914	435	5.53	20,771
iso-Hexane	C_6H_{14}	"	86.17	----	0.6527	140.4	442	902	438	5.48	20,743
N-Heptane	C_7H_{16}	"	100.20	----	0.6875	209.1	512	972	397	5.73	20,668
iso-Heptane	C_7H_{16}	"	100.20	----	0.6789	194.0	496	956	400	5.70	20,645
N-Octane	C_8H_{18}	"	114.22	----	0.7064	258.2	564	1,024	362	5.89	20,591
iso-Octane	C_8H_{18}	"	114.22	----	0.6918	210.5	546	1,006	373	5.80	20,556

* Compared with air = 1.   † Compared with water = 1.

Of the hydrocarbons containing five or more carbon atoms, only a few are shown; many isomers are known, as follows: 3 pentanes, 5 hexanes, 9 heptanes, 18 octanes. The iso-octane shown above is the one commonly used as the standard for rating "octane numbers" of gasolines. Its "octane" number is *100*.

have the same number of atoms in the molecule, but possess slightly different physical properties.

Natural gas occurs both in reservoirs that contain liquid
hydrocarbons and in those where no such liquids are present.
In the former case, all of the gas may be dissolved in the oil,
or if more gas is present than can dissolve in the oil at the particular conditions that prevail within the reservoir, a gas-cap may
be found above the oil zone. The special conditions that determine
the quantity of gas in solution are the pressure and temperature
of the reservoir, the quantities of gas and oil available, and their
respective chemical compositions. Of the many hydrocarbons that
make up natural gas, methane is the most abundant (Table III).

Gases are sometimes called wet or dry depending upon the
amount of liquid hydrocarbons that can be recovered from them
by various mechanical methods of processing, such as compression, cooling, or absorption in oil. Of the liquids so recovered,
the propane and butane fractions are in many instances separated
by further treatment and made available for use as special lique-
fied petroleum gases. These have become important as fuels for
domestic consumption and internal-combustion engines and as
the raw materials from which a host of industrial chemicals may
be manufactured.

Just as all inanimate matter obeys the physical laws of nature,
so the various hydrocarbons respond to changes in their physical
environment. Pure methane, the lightest hydrocarbon, is a gas at
ordinary pressure and temperature. If the pressure is raised to
500 pounds per square inch absolute (psia) and the temperature cooled to $-131°$ F., it becomes a liquid. Further cooling converts the liquid to a solid at a temperature of $-296°$ F. Similarly,
ethane, the second-lightest petroleum hydrocarbon, while a gas
at ordinary pressure and temperature, becomes a liquid when the
pressure is raised to approximately 500 psia at $60°$ F. Propane
liquefies at a pressure of 85 psia and a temperature of $60°$ F.
Butane condenses to a liquid at a pressure of 26 psia and a temperature of $60°$ F. Pentane and the other heavier hydrocarbons
are all liquid at ordinary pressures and temperatures.

TABLE III

ANALYSES OF NATURAL GASES FROM VARIOUS SOURCES

No.	Source	Year	Composition – Per Cent											
			CH_4 Methane	C_2H_6 Ethane	C_3H_8 Propane	C_4H_{10} n-Butane	C_4H_{10} iso-Butane	C_5H_{12} Pentane	C_6H_{14} Hexane	C_7H_{16} Heptane	CO_2 Carbon Dioxide	N_2 Nitrogen	H_2S Hydrogen Sulfide	O_2 Oxygen
1	Amarillo, Texas	1939	92.30	3.09	1.81	0.93†	---	0.56	---	---	---	1.59	---	0.22
2	Carthage, Texas	1944	90.12	4.03	1.52	0.73	0.36	0.50	0.16	0.25	0.60	1.73	---	---
3	Hugoton, Kansas	1947	75.80	6.22	3.82	1.04	0.46	0.49	0.28	---	0.20	11.69	tr.	---
4	Kettleman Hills, Calif.	1939	85.36	8.62	5.10	0.92†	---	---	---	---	---	---	---	---
5	North Pettus, Texas	1944	88.30	5.77	2.35	0.61	0.34	0.44	0.13	0.11	1.80	0.15	---	---
6	Okla. Nat. Gas Co.*	1949	82.52	8.20	3.67	1.86†	---	0.72	0.19	0.19	0.70	1.95	---	---
7	Rodessa, Louisiana	1939	84.67	6.08	2.34	0.82	0.64	0.53	0.29	0.12	0.50	4.01	---	---
8	Shuler, Arkansas	1938	73.46	11.51	5.07	2.33†	---	0.77	0.25	0.12	1.06	5.43	---	---
9	Walden, Colorado		0.52	3.95	---	---	---	---	---	---	92.14¶	3.16	---	0.09
10	West Cement, Okla.	1947	94.86	2.56	1.00	0.26	0.12	0.21	0.30‡	---	---	0.69	---	---
11	Worland, Wyoming	1950	58.90	6.10	1.90	0.60	0.40	0.40	0.40	---	2.70	---	28.6§	---

* Pipe-line gas.
† Includes all butanes.
‡ Includes hexanes and heavier.
¶ Total carbon dioxide 53 tons per million cubic feet.
§ Total sulfur 12 tons per million cubic feet.

28

Crude-oil Mixtures at Elevated Pressures

One of the most common sights in America today is a bottle of carbonated beverage. When the cap is removed from the bottle, bubbles rise to the surface of the liquid. Carbon-dioxide gas that had been dissolved in the liquid bubbles out of solution as the pressure falls when the bottle cap is removed. If the bottle of beverage is warmed, the pressure within the bottle increases. If the bottle cap is removed from the warmed bottle, the carbonated gas comes out of solution with such force that part of the beverage is lifted out of the bottle. This same principle is applicable to oil and gas mixtures under high pressures in the reservoir.

The behavior of oil and gas mixtures within the reservoir as production takes place is illustrated by use of a cylinder containing a sample of the mixture and a movable piston (Figure 22, View A).

To represent the reservoir before production begins, 1.620 barrels of reservoir liquid which has 1,200 standard cubic feet of gas dissolved in it is placed in the cylinder at a pressure of 3,000 psia and a temperature of 160° F. This mixture occupies 9.09 cubic feet of space under these conditions. The following changes occur when the piston is raised at constant temperature and the pressure on the mixture is permitted to decline:

Pressure on Mixture Psia	Space Occupied by Reservoir Liquid Cu. Ft.	Space Occupied by Free Gas Cu. Ft.	Cumulative Amount of Gas That Has Come Out of Solution St'd. Cu. Ft.	Figure 22 Views
3,000	9.09	---	---	A
2,900	9.15	Bubble-point	Bubble	B
2,400	8.69	1.04	168	C
2,000	8.36	2.24	300	D
1,600	8.01	4.19	400	E
1,130	7.63	8.28	600	F
500	7.05	25.96	820	G

If the original 9.09 cubic feet of reservoir oil and gas mixture are brought to surface conditions, atmospheric pressure of 14.65 psia and temperature of 60° F., the gas which comes out of solution

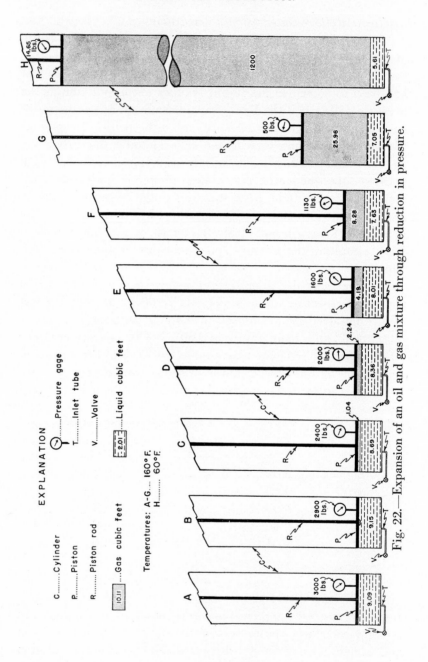

Fig. 22.—Expansion of an oil and gas mixture through reduction in pressure.

EXPLANATION

C........Cylinder

P........Piston

R........Piston rod

10.11 ....Gas cubic feet

⌀........Pressure gage

T........Inlet tube

V........Valve

2.01 ....Liquid cubic feet

Temperatures: A-G.... 160° F.
　　　　　　　H....... 60° F.

30

will occupy 1,200 cubic feet of space (Figure 22, View H) and the oil will occupy only 5.61 cubic feet, or one barrel. The liquid at these conditions is termed *residual oil* or *stock-tank oil*. In other words, what would appear to be almost two barrels of oil in a reservoir at 3,000 psia and 160° F. shrinks to only one barrel in the period during which the fluid travels from the porous reservoir rock to the stock tanks on top of the ground. The remainder of the original volume, 0.620 barrels, is the space in the reservoir liquid occupied by the gas that came out of solution.

Important changes in the physical properties of the reservoir petroleum and gas take place during the above process. The specific gravity, viscosity, and surface tension (the tendency for the surface of a liquid to behave as a thin elastic film) of the reservoir liquid are less than the corresponding properties of the surface or stock-tank oil. Lighter weight, lower viscosity, lower surface-tension oil will flow to the well bore more readily than it would if the light solution-gas were removed. Since these properties are dependent upon the amount of gas in solution, which in turn is dependent upon the reservoir pressure, the specific gravity, viscosity, and surface tension increase as the pressure on an oil and gas mixture are lowered (Figure 23).

Gas-condensate Mixtures at Elevated Pressures

In the gas-condensate mixture, the gas at high pressures is the solvent rather than the liquid. The gas carries in solution a part or all of the accompanying hydrocarbon liquid. The produced liquid generally has a high A. P. I. gravity and is water-white or pale straw-colored. Laboratory studies of the sample of reservoir fluid at temperatures and pressures similar to those in the reservoir, as well as a complete laboratory analysis to determine the amount and kind of the various hydrocarbons that make up the sample, are necessary to identify this type of reservoir.

The important difference between the gases and liquids or the gaseous and liquid phases (gas being one physical phase and liquid the other) is the degree of compressibility. In general, gases shrink to half their original volume when the pressure upon them is doubled. Conversely, gases expand as the pressure on them

31

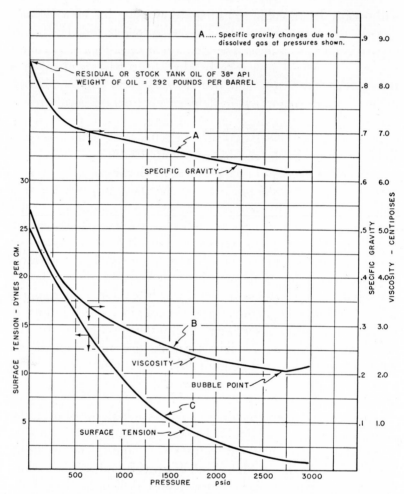

Fig. 23.—Effect of pressure changes on properties of reservoir oil.

is reduced (Figure 24). Liquids show very little change in volume even though the pressure may change enormously.

Under the very high temperatures and pressures that are present in some of the deep reservoirs, the physical properties of the gases and liquids are so nearly alike that it may be difficult to distinguish between them. The densities, viscosities, and surface tensions of the gas and liquid phases are nearly the same at high

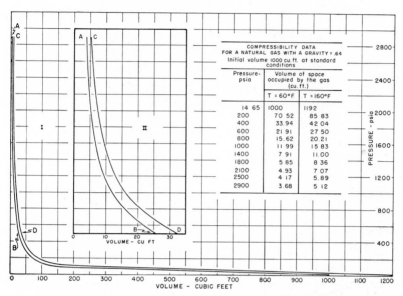

COMPRESSIBILITY DATA FOR A NATURAL GAS WITH A GRAVITY = .64 Initial volume 1000 cu.ft. at standard conditions		
Pressure- psia	Volume of space occupied by the gas (cu. ft.)	
	T = 60°F	T = 160°F
14 65	1000	1192
200	70 52	85 83
400	33.94	42 04
600	21 91	27 50
800	15.62	20.21
1000	11 99	15 83
1400	7 91	11.00
1800	5 85	8 36
2100	4.93	7 07
2500	4 17	5.89
2900	3.68	5 12

Fig. 24.—Expansion of gas through pressure reduction.
Graphs of inset II are enlargements of portions of Graphs I.
Expansion of gas at 60° F. shown by Curve A–B, at
160° F. by Curve C–D.

pressures and temperatures, and even the compressibilities become quite similar.

The change in densities (Figure 25) for a reservoir liquid and its associated gas-cap illustrates how elevated pressures remove any features which distinguish gases from liquids. As the reservoir pressure is increased, the density of the liquid petroleum in the reservoir decreases because of the gas that is forced into solution. The density of the gas-cap increases because it is compressed to a more confined space. Their densities become indistinguishable at 5,200 psia.

The behavior of gas-condensate mixtures within the reservoir as production takes place is also illustrated by use of a cylinder containing a sample of the mixture and a movable piston (Figure 26, View A). Release of pressure at constant temperature causes condensation of the liquid as soon as the upper dew-point pressure is reached (Figure 26, View B). The *dew point* is the

33

pressure at which liquid starts to form. Continued drop in pressure is accompanied by an increase in liquid volume to the point of maximum liquid formation (Figure 26, View C). Below this point, upon further drop in pressure, the amount of liquid decreases, on account of revaporization (Figure 26, View D). The decrease in the quantity of liquid persists as the pressure declines to the dew-point pressure, below which no more liquid forms (Figure 26, View E).

Lower temperatures usually cause increased condensation. However, the mass of rock that comprises the reservoir is enormous in comparison with the mass of gas present, so that the above-described changes all take place at practically the same temperature. Lower earth temperatures are encountered as the

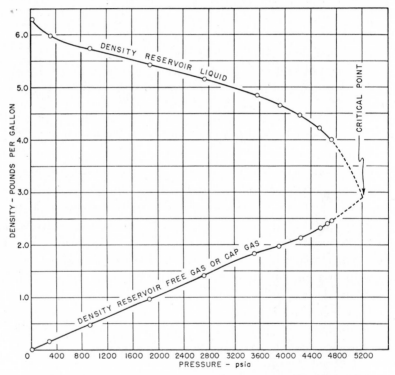

Fig. 25.—Changes in densities of a reservoir liquid (top) and its associated gas-cap (bottom) as pressures increase.

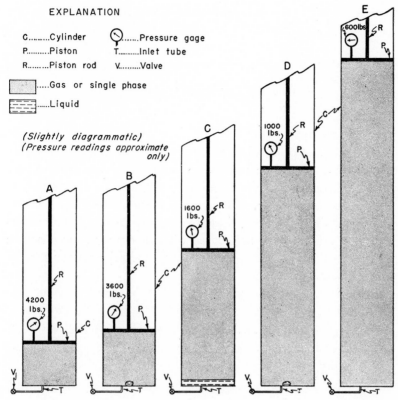

EXPLANATION

C.........Cylinder   ⌀......Pressure gage
P.........Piston   T..........Inlet tube
R.........Piston rod V.........Valve

▨.....Gas or single phase

▤......Liquid

(Slightly diagrammatic)
(Pressure readings approximate
only)

Fig. 26.—Expansion of a gas-condensate mixture through
pressure reduction.

stream of gas with its small quantity of condensate liquid moves
upward through the well flow string, and further liquid formation takes place.

The total fluid discharged at the wellhead then consists of gas,
condensate liquid that was formed either in the reservoir or in
the flow string, and small quantities of water condensed from the
vapor phase. A portion of the total liquid may also run back down
the walls of the pipe or remain in the reservoir where it adheres
to the mineral grains.

CHAPTER III

RESERVOIR MECHANICS

OIL RESERVOIRS

Oil does not produce itself. Crude oil as it exists at the surface possesses no energy with which to expel itself from the pores of a rock. If poured on a sandstone rock, it would be absorbed with little tendency for any to escape, even though the rock has porosity and permeability comparable to that of reservoir rock. It is necessary that crude oil be associated with an energy source before it can be moved into the bottom of a well and raised to the surface of the earth.

The sources of natural energy, one or more of which are present in all commercially productive oil reservoirs, are:

1. The expansion, as a result of pressure reduction, either of gas which has come out of solution from the reservoir oil or of free gas initially present in the reservoir;

2. edge or bottom water encroachment, also a result of reduction of pressure;

3. gravitational force; and

4. expansion of the reservoir oil itself as pressure is released.

Either gas expansion or water encroachment provides the principal energy for most petroleum reservoirs. Both become operative only with a release of pressure. A hole must be bored into the reservoir rock to release reservoir pressure. It provides a connection between the high-pressure oil reservoir and the low pressure existing at the earth's surface. The pressure release causes a pressure gradient within the reservoir toward the bottom of the well bore. Natural energy sources become active and move oil into the well bore, whence it is brought to the surface either through natural energy or by means of artificial lift. Some oil and gas reservoirs may contain large quantities of unrecoverable oil because they have no natural pressure and are not susceptible to the application of artificial recovery methods.

In Chapter II the solution of gas in oil under pressure was explained. Such gas is called *solution-gas*. Its expansion, after escape from solution in oil as pressures are released, provides energy for moving oil. An oil reservoir in which the energy for production of oil is obtained mainly from expansion of solution-gas is classified as one controlled by *solution-gas expansion*.

In those reservoirs where the volume of gas exceeds the amount dissolved in the oil, the excess gas exists in a free state as a *gas-cap* above the oil zone. If the oil in such a reservoir is withdrawn in a manner that permits the gas-cap to expand into the oil zone, the reservoir is said to be controlled by *gas-cap expansion*. The energy for producing oil in this type of reservoir comes from both expanding gas-cap gas and solution-gas as pressures are released.

Another source of natural energy in a reservoir comes from water which encroaches into the oil zone to flush oil from the reservoir rock and moves it to the wells where lower pressures prevail. Water can encroach from two sources:

1. A continuous reservoir horizon that outcrops some distance from the oil and gas reservoir acts as a conduit through which water under a hydraulic head encroaches on the oil and gas zone as pressures are released. Actual flow of water occurs in the reservoir horizon similar to the flow of water through artesian basins.

2. In some instances various geologic processes have combined to bury the outcrops of reservoir rocks under impervious beds of more recent time, and hence effectively prevent further entrance of water into the buried strata. However, the water within the buried layers would still be under a pressure of approximately forty-four pounds per square inch for each one hundred feet of depth. The compressibility of water is so small that it may be safely neglected in most calculations, but even though the change in volume of a barrel of water for each pound change in pressure is negligible, the over-all change in volume be-

37

comes a factor of great magnitude when the total volume of water is many billions of barrels and the pressure change is several hundred pounds or more. Under these conditions the compressed water behaves very much like a compressed steel spring that rebounds instantly when the weight on it is decreased slightly or removed entirely. Many reservoir rocks contain enormous quantities of water, so compressed that the drop in pressure that accompanies production of oil and gas is also attended by prompt expansion of the water, which keeps pace with the movement of the oil.

Both of the above processes are believed to be active in a number of producing reservoirs, with the net result that both artesian flow and expansion of compressed water provide the energy for production of the oil and gas. *Water-drive* is the term used to describe such reservoirs.

Gravitational force also supplies a source of energy for producing oil. It acts ceaselessly on the reservoir fluids in all types of reservoirs; but only where the permeability of the reservoir rock and structural dip are high or the sand is thick does it become active enough to furnish the primary driving force for production. Gravity-drainage reservoirs are those in which the movement of oil is controlled primarily by gravity.

If the pressure is greater than is necessary to force all the associated gas into solution, the oil is *undersaturated*. In such a reservoir, gas is released from solution in the oil after the reservoir pressure declines below the saturation pressure. Energy for initial production is obtained from the expansibility of the reservoir oil itself. Common usage has classified such reservoirs as *undersaturated*—a classification based upon a condition of the reservoir oil rather than the controlling energy source. As the pressure falls below the saturation pressure, expansion of the solution-gas becomes the producing energy and the reservoir converts to the solution-gas expansion type.

Gas under pressure can be returned to the oil reservoir through well bores to create a pressure differential between different parts of the reservoir. Water also is frequently injected into reservoirs to create a pressure differential and supply additional energy. In many instances as much oil has been recovered by these secondary operations as was originally produced by depletion of the natural pressure.

The Solution-gas Expansion Reservoir

The most common type of oil reservoir is the one controlled by solution-gas expansion. This type is also called a *volumetrically* controlled reservoir because the pressure reduction is directly dependent on the volume of fluids produced. All primary forces may be present and act on the fluids in the reservoir, but the solution-gas energy is dominant. A source of water energy might be available and the field still be controlled by solution-gas expansion if the rate of production should exceed the rate at which water enters the oil reservoir, or if all encroaching water were produced by edge wells.

When a solution-gas expansion reservoir is produced at capacity, the producing rate declines according to a particular trend (Figure 27). When it is restricted or prorated, the producing rate does not decline until after the restricted production rate equals the capacity of the field to produce. The characteristic pressure decline in a solution-gas expansion reservoir as oil and gas are produced is shown by Figure 28, Curve A.

A very rapid pressure drop takes place during the early life of an undersaturated reservoir when expansion of the oil furnishes the energy for production (Figure 28, Curve B). After the pressure declines to the saturation point, solution-gas energy becomes operative and pressure then takes the characteristic decline. The relative positions of Curves A and B on Figure 28 have no comparative significance with respect to the recovery to be expected from saturated or undersaturated reservoirs.

Gas-oil ratios (the number of cubic feet of gas per barrel of oil) increase during the early life of the field and decline during the stripper stage of production (Figure 28, Curve C).

A lenticular, solution-gas expansion reservoir produces little, if any, water. Over their entire producing life, wells in this type of reservoir may produce from 1 to 5 per cent water if the connate

39

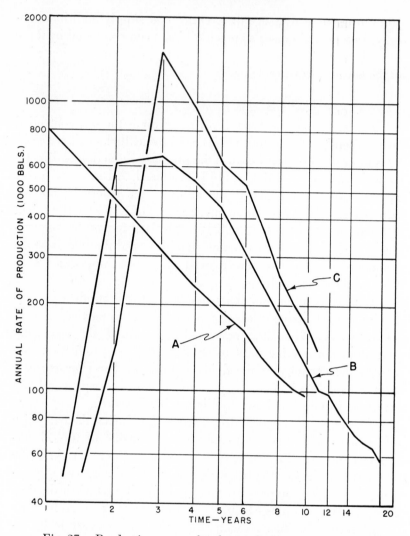

Fig. 27.—Production curves for three solution-gas expansion reservoirs. When the rate of production declines, the logarithm of the rate of production plotted against the logarithm of time is approximately a straight line. Curve A for reservoir fully developed first year after discovery, B for reservoir developed second year, and C for third year.

40

water content is from 40 to 50 per cent. Such water furnishes no energy for the production of oil. It is merely contained in the pore space along with the oil in sufficient amounts to be produced.

Some reservoirs cover a large area and have a low rate of water encroachment. If the rate of production exceeds the rate of water encroachment, they are controlled by solution-gas expansion, and wells at the water-oil contact produce large quantities of water.

The volume of oil recoverable by solution-gas expansion, including not only the volume recovered during the flowing life of the field but also that obtained during the pumping life, may vary from 10 to 35 per cent of the original oil-in-place. A part of the 65 to 90 per cent of the original oil remaining in the reservoir can sometimes be recovered by secondary operations if such methods can be applied economically.

Greater ultimate recovery from solution-gas expansion reservoirs is brought about by restricted production rates only if advantage is taken of a second and more efficient source of natural energy. Restricted production rates from a reservoir with good permeability and structural relief may permit gravity forces to become effective enough to change the production control from solution-gas expansion to a combination of solution-gas expansion and gravity drainage. The latter provides more efficient drainage and results in greater oil recovery. Because gravity drainage tends to segregate the oil and gas in the reservoir, those wells completed, or recompleted, below the gas-oil contact obtain more oil production. A solution-gas expansion reservoir with a partial water-drive may yield greater oil recovery if production rates are so restricted as to permit efficient washing of the sand by the encroaching water. Unless wells at or near the water-oil contact are produced at a restricted rate, fingering of the encroaching water will trap and make unrecoverable large volumes of oil (Figure 32, View B).

Gas-oil ratios of different wells in the same reservoir vary considerably. A limit placed on the amount of oil produced from high-ratio wells fosters a greater ultimate oil recovery from the reservoir as a whole and prevents voidage of disproportionate

41

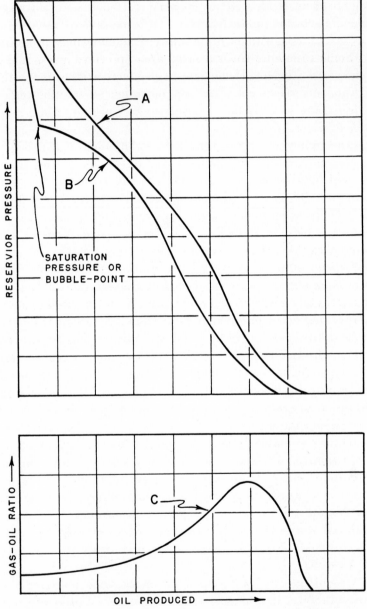

Fig. 28.—Generalized pressure decline and gas-oil ratio curves for solution-gas expansion reservoirs.

amounts of reservoir space. High-ratio wells will void a greater space in the reservoir per barrels of oil produced. When they are unrestricted, or operated at a rate of oil production equal to that of the low-ratio wells, a low-pressure area is formed to which gas and oil will migrate from other parts of the common reservoir. High gas-oil ratios usually indicate inefficient use of natural gas. A limit can be placed on the amount of gas and oil each well may produce which will tend to preserve solution-gas energy in the reservoir that can later be utilized by the more efficient low gas-oil ratio wells.

The Combination Solution-gas Expansion, Gas-cap Expansion, and Gravity-drainage Reservoir

Solution-gas expansion, gas-cap expansion, and gravity drainage are sometimes treated as three distinct types of reservoir control. All three forces are usually active in any reservoir, even though one may predominate during different stages in its life. Gas-cap expansion and gravity drainage are most active in those reservoirs of marked structural relief, considerable sand thickness, and good permeability. The reservoir may or may not have an initial gas-cap. If one is present, it will expand into the space vacated by the oil as the oil moves down structure. Even though a gas-cap is absent at the date of discovery, gas liberated from solution will migrate to the vacated oil space on the top of the structure to form a gas-cap which expands as oil is produced.

Both the energy from an expanding gas-cap and that supplied from expanding solution-gas are the result of pressure decline. The force of gravity drainage is most effective in those reservoirs whose permeability is high enough to permit an economic rate of movement of fluids to the low part of the structure.

The performance of the gas-cap expansion type of reservoir depends upon the method of operation. A reservoir with a gas-cap equal in volume to that of the oil zone would have gas-oil ratio and pressure-performance histories similar to those illustrated by Curves C and D, Figure 29, provided all of the gas could be utilized for oil production. For comparison, Curves A and B, Figure 29, show the history of a reservoir without a gas-cap. In

43

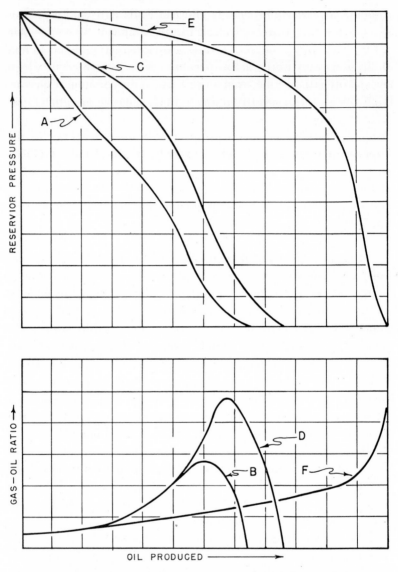

Fig. 29.—Pressure decline Curve A and gas-oil ratio Curve B of a reservoir without a gas-cap. Similar Curves C and D of a reservoir with a gas-cap equal in size to the oil zone. Curves E and F of a reservoir with a gas-cap equal in size to the oil zone, in which advantage is taken of gravity forces.

order to utilize the maximum energy of the gas-cap and obtain the greatest oil recovery, wells must be completed below the gas-oil contact and produce gas-cap gas only after it has passed through the oil zone. Practical considerations, such as lease boundaries and obligations, prevent this kind of operation in most oil fields. A reservoir with a gas-cap equal in size to the oil zone, in which advantage is also taken of gravity forces, would have a performance history as typified by Curves E and F, Figure 29. Increased oil recovery of approximately 50 to 75 per cent over that obtained from a field without any gas-cap could be realized. Again, proper completion of wells so as to produce below the gas-oil contact is necessary, and proper operational controls must be placed upon the various wells dependent upon their structural position.

When the pressure of the gas-cap is depleted faster than that of the oil zone, the resulting pressure difference stimulates upward movement of both solution-gas and oil into the gas-cap. Capillary forces enable the pore spaces of the gas-cap rock to retain liquids that migrate into them. Consequently some of the oil which moves from the oil zone to the gas-cap is made unrecoverable. As the oil in the oil zone loses its solution-gas to the gas-cap, the remainder of the oil becomes less mobile and a large portion of it is rendered unrecoverable.

Factors which influence the recovery of oil are the structural position of the producing wells, rates of production, and completion methods. If production rates are so restricted as to permit the fluids to separate in the reservoir, the migration of oil and solution-gas to the gas-cap will be negligible.

The Water-drive Reservoir

The performance of water-drive reservoirs is typified by a slight decline in pressure, very little change in producing gas-oil ratios, and a steady increase in the volume of water produced per well. The first water production comes from those wells near the water-oil contact. As the reservoir is depleted, the water-oil contact moves up structure. Eventually water is produced from all wells in the reservoir.

45

In reservoirs where water underlies the entire oil zone, as in some dome-type structures, the water table may rise uniformly from the base to the top of the structure, floating the oil to the wells higher on structure as the reservoir is produced. Water may also encroach laterally through the most permeable streaks to be produced in the high-structure wells, or it may encroach in a combination of these two ways.

Some control on water production can be accomplished by selective recompletion of the wells. Zones that produce water can be plugged off, and zones not previously flooded can be opened. If wells are produced at excessive rates, the water will find channels toward the well opening and much of the oil will be left behind. Oil may ride the top of the water and be *coned off* (Figure 30), or the oil in the relatively impermeable streaks may be *by-passed* (Figure 31) and leave large quantities of oil unrecoverable.

Recovery of oil from water-drive reservoirs depends upon the amount of water-coning or by-passing. Under ideal reservoir conditions, as much as 85 per cent of the oil content may be recov-

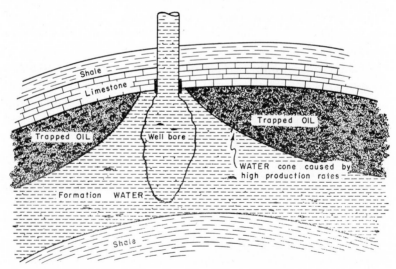

Fig. 30.—Oil coned off by water as a result of excessive production rates.

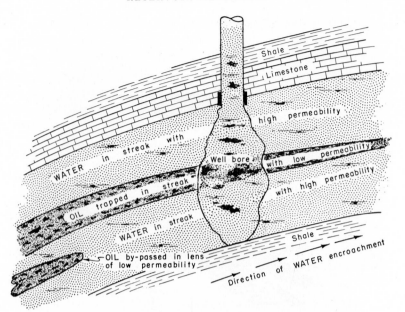

Fig. 31.—Oil trapped in streaks of low permeability as water
by-passes them. Excessive production rates cause the water to
follow only the streaks of high permeability.

ered from zones through which the water passes. But the total
recovery depends upon the character of the reservoir rock, on the
oil itself, and also on the nature of the production controls designed to prevent excessive by-passing. Estimates of such recoveries usually range from 40 to 70 per cent of the initial oil-in-
place.

A water-drive reservoir produced at rates which permit but a
slight drop in pressure generally realizes the greatest ultimate
recovery. Instances occur where it is necessary to create a rather
large pressure differential before the water-drive becomes an
active force in recovery of the oil.

Practical Aspects of Primary Producing Forces

A stratigraphic-type reservoir in its initial or discovery condition is illustrated in Figure 32, View A. This trap is fairly persistent and is connected to a source of water energy. The reservoir

47

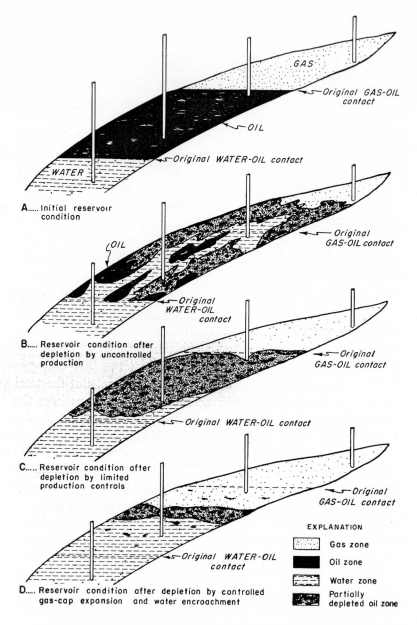

GAS

Original GAS-OIL
contact

OIL

Original WATER-OIL contact

WATER

A.....Initial reservoir
condition

OIL

Original
GAS-OIL contact

Original
WATER-OIL
contact

B..... Reservoir condition after
depletion by uncontrolled
production

Original
GAS-OIL contact

Original WATER-OIL contact

C..... Reservoir condition after
depletion by limited
production controls

Original
GAS-OIL contact

EXPLANATION

Gas zone

Oil zone

Water zone

Partially
depleted oil zone

Original WATER-OIL
contact

D..... Reservoir condition after depletion by controlled
gas-cap expansion and water encroachment

Fig. 32.—Sketches that show how oil recoveries increase in
a water-drive reservoir if production rates are controlled.

rock has considerable dip and good permeability. The oil in the reservoir is saturated with gas and a gas-cap is present.

If each well in this reservoir were produced wide open, much oil otherwise recoverable would be left in the reservoir. Uncontrolled production of wells completed in the gas-cap would develop a low pressure therein, so that oil would move into the gas-cap. A significant amount of oil would be made unrecoverable by *wetting* the gas-cap rock and wasting the energy of the gas-cap. The water-drive would be ineffective since production by the down-structure wells would make it impossible for the encroaching water to keep up with the rate of oil production. The reservoir would not be controlled by water-drive, but by solution-gas expansion, because the method of operation would compel it to be so. A reasonable estimate of ultimate recovery by such a method of operation is 15 to 25 per cent of the initial oil-in-place. Distribution of fluids in the reservoir when further production is uneconomical would be as shown in Figure 32, View B.

The reservoir could produce as a solution-gas expansion type under certain restrictions and recover greater oil volume. If all wells in the field were restricted to rates of production that voided equal volumes of reservoir space, there would be less tendency for oil to move up structure and be left in the originally dry gas-cap. Approximately 20 to 30 per cent of the original oil-in-place could be recovered and the reservoir left in the condition as shown by Figure 32, View C.

The same reservoir could be produced under solution-gas expansion and gas-cap expansion and recover 30 to 45 per cent of the oil if (1) all gas wells were shut in and (2) oil wells completed below the gas-oil contact and those at the water-oil contact produced only enough water to prevent water encroachment on the oil zone.

A greater recovery could be realized from a reservoir of this type if oil production and gas production were both strictly controlled. The reservoir would be a combination water-drive and gas-cap expansion reservoir if gas wells were shut in, high gas-oil ratio wells were restricted, and the combined rate of oil and gas production from wells in all parts of the reservoir limited to the rate at which water entered the reservoir. In this operation 45 to 75 per cent of the oil-in-place could be recovered and the reservoir left similar to that shown by Figure 32, View D. Such efficient operations are feasible only where the owners of wells on individual tracts agree that production shall be taken from those wells which are located most advantageously on the structure.

Secondary Energy for Production

In most oil reservoirs, natural energy for production can be supplemented to bring about increased oil recovery by injection of either gas or water into the reservoir. If such injection takes place while the reservoir pressures are still high and most of the wells still flowing, the operation is classified as *pressure maintenance*. If it is started after pressures have been substantially depleted and the field is in the general pumping or stripper stage, it is classified as *secondary recovery, repressuring,* or *water-flooding*.

Vacuum applied at the wellhead permits utilization of more of the energy of the gas initially present by lowering the abandonment pressure and also effects additional oil recovery. But vacuum applied prior to gas or water injection may be detrimental to recovery of oil because it may leave the reservoir oil in a more viscous condition.

In *gas-injection operations*, wet gas produced with the oil is taken from separators and transported through a gas-gathering system to a gasoline plant where the liquefiable hydrocarbons are removed. After these liquid hydrocarbons have been removed, the *dry-gas*, sometimes called *residue gas*, is compressed and returned to the reservoir through input wells to maintain pressure.

In some oil fields where the gas contains an insufficient amount of liquefiable hydrocarbons to justify a *gasoline* plant, it is taken directly to a *gas-compression* plant. The residue-gas volume may be as much as 80 to 90 per cent of the produced-gas volume when handled through a compression plant. Such a plant does not extract much of the liquefiable hydrocarbons, and fuel requirements are low. As little as 70 per cent of the wet gas put through a gasoline plant may be returned as residue because a greater amount of the liquefiable hydrocarbons is removed and fuel requirements are large.

In some gas-injection operations make-up gas or gas produced from other reservoirs is purchased. This practice permits the injection of a gas volume equal to 100 per cent or more of the produced-gas volume. The result may be a true pressure-maintenance operation rather than the retarded pressure-depletion operation which takes place when only produced gas is returned to the reservoir. If input wells are grouped on the high part of the structure and gas injected into the gas-cap, the oil recovery will be increased. The gas-cap will expand and the oil zone contract as production takes place.

Gas-oil ratios increase slowly if the producing interval in each well is below the gas-oil contact and if the production rate is controlled to permit segregation of the gas and oil zones. When the oil column becomes thin, it will no longer be possible to prevent the entry of gas-cap gas to the well bore and ratios will increase rapidly. By that time, however, a substantial portion of the initial oil-in-place will have been recovered. Where surface ownership must be considered, the injection and producing wells cannot be located in the most advantageous part of the reservoir.

The viscosity of the oil in the reservoir, as compared to that of the gas, plays an important part not only in the oil recovered but also in the rate at which it is produced. Reservoir-oil viscosity and surface tension are least at the highest pressures. The more viscous the reservoir oil, the smaller the volume recovered and the lower the rate at which it may be withdrawn. Retention of gas in solution prevents an increase in the reservoir-oil viscosity and permits a higher rate of oil production as well as a greater ultimate recovery. The greatest increase in oil recovery can be obtained only when the injection operations are started early in the life of the field and the greatest volumes of gas are returned. The project may fail if gas injection is delayed to that late stage when gas production is negligible and no make-up gas is available for purchase. Oil recoveries from gas-cap pressure-maintenance operations increase in the order of 100 per cent over recoveries resulting from solution-gas expansion alone.

51

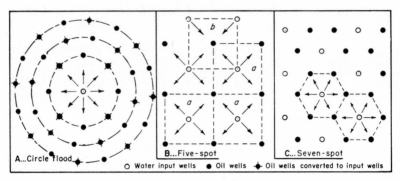

Fig. 33.—Three types of water-flood patterns.

As early as 1880, Pennsylvania producers discovered that an increase in oil recovery could be obtained by injection of water into oil reservoirs (*water-flooding*). The first water floods were probably caused by casing leaks opposite water-bearing sands. Such floods are commonly called *dump floods* and can effect an increase in recovery. Quite often, however, they trap large quantities of otherwise recoverable oil and are justifiable only when the economics of operation prevents the use of a carefully planned flood.

In some reservoirs water may be injected into wells located down structure and the oil floated to the producing wells. This is possible when reservoir-oil viscosities are low and the formation-rock permeabilities are high enough to permit the entire reservoir to be flooded within a reasonable period of time. When pressures have been depleted, the high viscosity of the reservoir oil usually requires that one of the *spot* flood patterns (Figure 33) be adopted in order to flood the reservoir economically.

Water injected continuously into a reservoir moves progressively away from the bore hole of the input well toward the producing well. An oil bank is created ahead of the advancing water front as it moves through the oil zone (Figures 34 and 35).

Several factors may contribute to the failure of a water flood. A failure may occur if the reservoir rock has such extreme variations in permeability that high water-oil ratios occur early in the life of the flood. When the connate water saturation is high, it may be impossible for the injected water to build up the oil bank and remove additional oil from the sand. If the oil zone is underlaid by a water zone from which it cannot be separated, a failure may occur because injected water enters a water zone more easily than it enters an oil zone. Slow movement of oil in the oil zone and rapid cycling of water through the water zone causes an early abandonment of the flood.

NATURAL GAS AND GAS-CONDENSATE RESERVOIRS

The previous discussion has dealt with those reservoirs from which oil production is the primary consideration, while the associated gas production is incidental and usually of less economic importance. It has been shown that the gas produced from some oil reservoirs was originally in solution in the oil and the mixture in a liquid state underground. In others, a gas-cap existed over the liquid oil in the high parts of the structure.

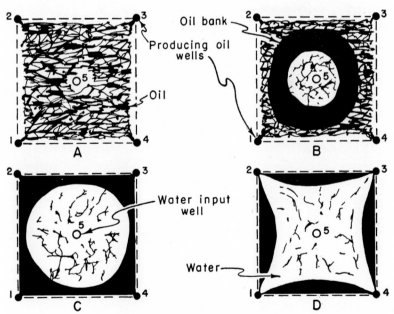

Fig. 34.—Horizontal views showing the progress of water through a formation with uniform porosity, permeability, and thickness.

Many reservoirs contain only gas and no oil, or the oil column, if present, is so thin or small as to be of no commercial significance. The sources of energy available to produce the gas from these reservoirs are similar to those active in oil reservoirs—gas expansion and water encroachment. Wells in gas fields which produce by the gas-expansion mechanism lose productive capacity as the pressure declines and are abandoned when they can no longer produce enough gas to pay the expense of operation. Where an active water-drive is present, the wells are progressively flooded out as the water migrates up structure.

Dry natural gas reservoirs are those in which the gas as produced contains no commercially recoverable liquids. However, some natural gas reservoirs produce gas from which a colorless volatile liquid can be obtained if the gas is cooled and passed through a separator or processed through a plant. From relatively

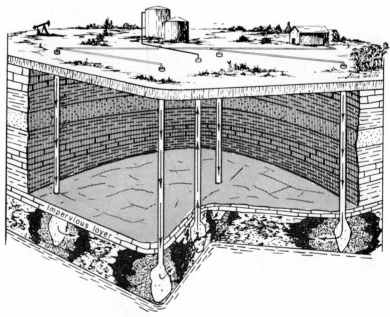

Fig. 35.—Three-dimensional view of five-spot flood, showing the progress of the water through a formation with uniform porosity, permeability, and thickness, when the center well is the producing well.

shallow gas fields where the original pressures are less than 1,500 to 2,000 pounds per square inch, the plant product extracted from the gas is called *natural gasoline*. The quantity recoverable from such low-pressure fields remains relatively constant throughout the productive life of the wells. On the other hand, the composition and quantity of the natural gasoline extracted from gas produced with crude petroleum changes over the life of the field.

A comparatively recent development in the gas-production phase of the petroleum industry has been the recognition and rise to economic importance of the *retrograde gas-condensate* or *gas-distillate* type of reservoir. Fields of this type were first recognized in the nineteen thirties as deeper drilling resulted in the discovery of sands with relatively high subsurface pressures and temperatures. Among the early fields of the retrograde gas-condensate type were Cotton Valley in Louisiana and Big Lake, La Blanca, and Agua Dulce in Texas.

With increased depth of drilling the trend is toward more frequent discovery of gas reservoirs. It is quite noticeable in the Gulf Coast region (Figure 36). In this area the ratio rises from approximately one gas reservoir to two oil reservoirs at a depth of less than 4,000 feet to a ratio of two gas reservoirs to one oil reservoir at a depth of approximately 10,000 feet.

Gas-condensate reservoirs have become more important because average well depths are greater. At the same time, economic problems arise because deep wells are expensive and the income per acre from a gas-condensate reservoir usually is less than from an oil reservoir. A proper understanding of the characteristics of this type of reservoir and the principles to be applied in their operation is essential.

The reduction in the quantity of condensate recovered from the La Blanca field as pressures declined is shown in Figure 37. The decline in liquid yield was due to condensation in the reservoir of some of the heavier hydrocarbons originally dissolved in gas. The condensed liquid was retained by the sand with the result that the produced gas was less rich in liquid hydrocarbons. It should be noted especially that the transformation of a liquid to a gas through reduction in pressure is the normal process, while

55

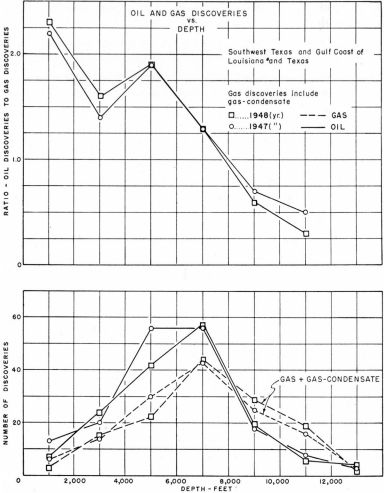

Fig. 36.—Comparison of oil and gas discoveries in Gulf Coast area.

formation of a liquid from a gas as the pressure falls is a phenomenon termed *retrograde condensation.*

The fact that a liquid condenses in the formation as pressure declines may be for most purposes a sufficiently good definition of retrograde condensation. However, occasions arise that require a more technical knowledge of the behavior of the gas-condensate mixture in the formation. Furthermore, it is not always practical or desirable to reduce the reservoir pressure sufficiently to determine whether retrograde condensation will occur. At best it would be a wasteful procedure since the liquid so condensed is to a large extent not recoverable. Fortunately, underground conditions can be simulated in the laboratory and observations made on a small scale. Furthermore, testing and laboratory procedures have been developed to such a point that reliable predictions of fluid behavior in the reservoir can be made from laboratory data.

The following procedure is used to procure a sample of the gas-condensate and examine it:

1. Condition the well so that fluid representative of the reservoir mixture enters the well bore and is produced at the surface.

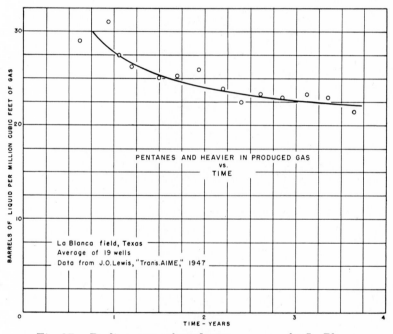

Fig. 37.—Decline curve of condensate recovery for La Blanca field, Texas. (Reproduced by permission of the publishers from James O. Lewis, "Interpretation of Well Test Data in Gas-condensate Fields," Trans. AIME (1947) 170, *Petroleum Development and Technology,* 202.)

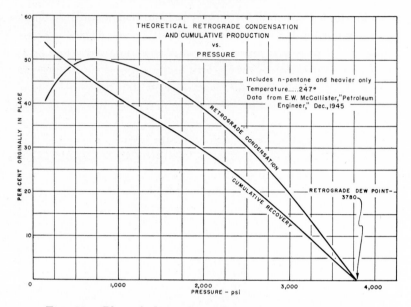

Fig. 38.—Plot of data obtained from typical laboratory examination of gas-condensate mixture. The condensate liquid content of the gas increases as the pressure falls to approximately 750 psia.

2. Segregate the produced fluids into a gas and a liquid.
3. Measure the relative amounts of gas and liquid produced.
4. Take samples of the segregated gas and liquid.
5. Recombine, in the laboratory, these samples of gas and liquid in the same proportions as they are produced.
6. Observe the behavior of the recombined samples at pressures and temperatures similar to those in the reservoir.

The results of a typical laboratory examination as discussed in Chapter II are shown in Figure 38. At reservoir temperature and pressure, the material is all in the gas phase and no liquid is present. Then, as gas is withdrawn and pressure in the laboratory container declines, a liquid condenses. The quantity of liquid increases as the pressure falls to approximately 750 psia and then decreases as partial revaporization takes place with further reduction in pressure. Briefly, the conclusion to be drawn from the laboratory study is that if this field were produced by the gas-expansion mechanism down to a pressure of 500 psia, only 49 per cent of the normal pentanes and heavier hydrocarbons would be recovered. The balance would remain in the unproduced gas phase or be retained as a liquid within the reservoir rock.

Some general observations concerning gas-condensate and the retrograde process are as follows:

1. The condensate, as produced in a conventional separator, is water-white to light straw in color. Its gravity is generally above 50° A.P.I. A large percentage (often above 50 per cent) of the condensate is within the boiling range of gasoline.

2. The ratio of gas produced to liquid condensate recovered in a conventional separator is usually between 10,000 and 100,000 cubic feet of gas per barrel of condensate (or between 100 barrels and 10 barrels of liquid per million cubic feet of gas).

3. Retrograde gas-condensate may occur in reservoirs with pressures as low as 1,500 psia but is usually found at pressures above 4,000 psia.

4. As compared with a crude-oil solution-gas mixture, gas-condensate is richer in methane, ethane, and propane—the light gaseous hydrocarbons. It is less rich in hydrocarbons heavier than hexane.

5. The amount of liquid made unrecoverable by retrograde condensation caused through pressure reduction ranges from a negligible amount up to 50 to 60 per cent of that originally present in the gas-condensate mixture.

Where economically feasible, maximum recovery of gas-condensate may be obtained by:

1. use of more efficient extraction methods than mechanical separation alone in order to recover a larger fraction of the light liquefiable hydrocarbons such as propane, butane, and pentane; and

2. minimizing the retrograde loss in the reservoir through maintenance of pressure.

Methods of Extraction

Liquids can be extracted from gas-condensate produced at the well either by mechanical separation or by plant processing.

Mechanical separation is achieved by means of a separator which may operate at pressures from 100 psia to more than 1,000 psia. The separator is operated at the pressure which will yield the maximum recovery from a specific gas-condensate mixture. Increased recovery is frequently obtained by means of *stage separation,* where the well stream is passed through two or more separators operated at different individual pressures.

The efficiency of mechanical separation may be improved, within limits, by control of temperature. Higher recoveries are obtained at lower temperatures. However, *gas hydrates* (similar to frost or ice) form at low temperatures, and it is usually necessary to remove the water from the gas if the separator is operated at low temperatures.

More efficient and complete recovery can be obtained by plant processing in which the liquids are removed by absorption in an oil. Many of the absorptive-type plants in operation recover from the wet gas more than 30 per cent of propane, 80 per cent of the butanes, and practically all of the pentanes, hexanes, heptanes, and heavier hydrocarbons. The dry residue gas from the plants is composed of methane, ethane, propane, some butane, and very little, if any, pentanes and heavier hydrocarbons.

The following table presents a comparison of the results of the various extraction methods applied to typical gas-condensate:

	Conventional Separation	Multi-stage Separation	Plant Extraction
Barrels of liquid per million cubic feet of retrograde gas	52	58	70
A.P.I. gravity of recovered liquid, degrees	54.7	58.4	64.4

The increase in recovery through plant processing is due in large part to increased recovery of propanes, butanes, and pentanes, all of which are quite volatile, high A.P.I. gravity liquids. The above table shows that the increased recoveries of these light hydrocarbons raise the average gravity of the recovered liquid from 54.7 to 64.4° A.P.I.

Cycling

The gas and liquid recoveries from a natural gas reservoir are dependent on the original reservoir pressure and the pressure remaining when the field is abandoned. Recoveries of more than 75 per cent of the gas and liquid originally in place can be obtained if the original pressure is high (1,000 psia, for instance) and the abandonment pressure is low (250 psia). Where an active water-drive exists, recoveries up to 90 per cent of the amount originally in place may be obtained.

The recovery of gas by depletion from gas-condensate reservoirs also depends on the initial and final pressures. However, because of retrograde condensation, the percentage of condensate recovery may be substantially lower than that of the gas. Where the retrograde loss is sufficiently large and where there is little water-drive, the losses may be minimized by maintaining reservoir pressure.

Cycling is a form of pressure maintenance applied to gas-condensate reservoirs. The liquid hydrocarbons are removed from the rich gas produced; the residue or dry gas is compressed and injected through other wells into the same reservoir from which it was produced. The volume of gas injected amounts to 80 to 90 per cent of the volume of gas produced. The difference is due to the shrinkage caused by extraction of liquids and the use of gas for plant fuel. Thus the net withdrawal of gas from the reservoir is low for each barrel of condensate recovered, and the reservoir pressure declines at a low rate.

Cycling-plant gas capacity ranges from less than 15 million cubic feet per day to that of the plant (Figure 39) in the Katy field, Texas, which is rated at 450 million cubic feet per day.

In a cycled reservoir the injected dry gas eventually displaces the rich gas, and the gas from the producing wells begins to *dry up*. When the point is reached where earnings from recovered liquids no longer justify continued operation, the cycling operation is abandoned, and the field may be produced as a source of natural gas.

It is estimated that 60 to 80 per cent of the condensate in some reservoirs can be obtained by cycling. Cycling, followed by gas sales, may result in recoveries up to 90 per cent of the condensate originally in place.

On account of the lack of a suitable market for the residue gas, cycling may be utilized as a method for recovering the liquids while storing the gas for future sale, even though cycling may not be needed in order to maintain the pressure.

The cycling process is not applicable to some gas-condensate reservoirs for a number of reasons:

    1. The losses by retrograde condensation may be so small or the reservoir may be so small that the additional recovery obtainable by cycling would not justify the expenditures

Fig. 39.—View of cycling plant, Katy field, Texas; the largest cycling plant in the world.

required to drill the wells, build the plant, and operate the project.

2. Faults, shale breaks, or large variations in permeability may divide the field into a number of small reservoirs, and injected gas will not effectively displace rich gas or maintain pressure.

3. The capacities of the wells to produce may be too small to furnish sufficient rich gas for economic operation of a minimum-size cycling plant.

4. A water-drive may be present that will maintain pressure and make cycling unnecessary.

5. Ordinarily the cycling of gas-condensates containing less than twenty to twenty-five barrels of liquid per million cubic feet of gas is not feasible unless the gas-condensate reservoir is large.

If cycling is not necessary or practicable, the residue gas may be utilized for several purposes: (1) injection into an oil reservoir in order to maintain pressure and increase oil recovery, (2) injection for storage in another gas reservoir, or (3) sale to gas-transmission lines. Any of these methods may be used in conjunction with return of part of the produced gas to the reservoir.

If a reservoir is to be cycled, unitization is necessary for maximum recovery and efficient operation. The portion of the reservoir occupied by the dry gas is not determined by lease lines, but by the following factors:

1. shape or geometry of the reservoir and location of the producing or injection wells therein;

2. rates per well at which gas is produced or injected;

3. section of the reservoir exposed to the well bore; and

4. variations in permeability, porosity, water saturation, and sand thickness.

Control of the cycling project is achieved through operation of the wells. It is axiomatic that the wells should originally be placed in the most favorable locations. The number of wells is important only up to a minimum which must be determined for each reservoir; above this minimum no increase in recovery will be obtained by drilling additional wells. Average well spacings of considerably more than 640 acres per well are common in cycling operations.

The rates of production per well range up to 25 million cubic feet a day for production; injection rates are greater. Control of the rates per well is essential to good operation of a cycling project.

Gas Sales

If a gas reservoir is not cycled, or after cycling has become uneconomical, the gas may be sold. The available gas market or outlet is usually prorated where total well capacity exceeds the market demand. Some of the factors used in allocating the production are acreage, open-flow potential, closed-in wellhead pressure, and sand thickness. Wells are always produced at less than the open-flow potential because of the back pressure carried on the flow line. In some states the wells are limited to a maximum of 25 per cent of the open-flow potential.

WELL SPACING

Well spacing deals with the number of and distance between wells drilled to produce either oil or gas from a common source of supply. In the early days of the industry, wells were drilled on any surface tract, no matter how small. Some fields were developed in which it was possible to move from well to another by walking across derrick floors. This practice resulted in a waste of materials and oil.

Most of the new oil and gas fields are developed on a uniform well spacing with nearly equal distances between all wells. Generally oil reservoirs are developed with a well to each 10, 20, 40, or 80 acres, and gas fields with a well on each 160 to 640 acres. Gas reservoirs can be drained by fewer wells than oil reservoirs.

The ultimate oil recovery depends primarily on proper well completions, rates of production, and restriction of gas-oil and water-oil ratios. Regardless of spacing, much oil is left unrecoverable in the reservoir if these factors are improperly controlled.

In many fields proper location with reference to the geological structure is necessary for the greatest ultimate oil recovery. In gas-cap expansion reservoirs, wells concentrated low on the structure take advantage of both gas-cap expansion and gravity drainage. Few, if any, wells need be located in the up-structure gas-cap area. In water-drive reservoirs, wells concentrated near the crest of the structure produce water-free oil for the longest time.

For proper reservoir control in new fields it is important to determine as promptly as possible the structure, the reservoir-rock characteristics, the extent of the reservoir, the magnitude of reserves, the primary reservoir-energy source, and the type of reservoir control which will permit the greatest recovery. These data can best be determined by drilling new fields on the widest practical spacing pattern. Wide-spacing-development programs afford information that may be used to locate the most advantageous structural position for the drilling of future infill wells and eliminate the expense of drilling many unnecessary wells. Each reservoir presents a separate problem in the determination of the well-spacing pattern.

Unit Operation

An oil or gas reservoir is a natural unit in which the common supply of oil and gas accumulated during geologic periods without respect to surface property lines and fences. The reservoir is like an open range, but, unlike cattle, the oil and gas can be neither branded nor confined to their original boundaries by means of fences.

In the early days of the petroleum industry owners knew only what could be observed on the surface of the earth. They could only speculate on conditions in the subsurface reservoir as oil and gas were withdrawn. The realization that offset wells drained oil from adjacent properties stimulated the drilling of additional wells. This established a drilling pattern whereby each operator was forced to match the conduct of the offset operator in order to protect his own rights. The pattern required that wells be offset directly and that leases be drilled with approximately equal well densities. The apparent protection against drainage actually resulted in waste of gas, of reservoir energy, and of materials, as well as a reduction in total recoverable oil.

As various governmental bodies, both state and national, began to comprehend the importance of the conservation of our natural resources, many state regulatory bodies were empowered to promulgate and enforce some degree of uniform and regular well spacing. For the most part, production was still shared on the basis of surface area or lease boundaries, but no operator was permitted to place another in a position of hardship by forcing him to waste money and material in the drilling of unnecessary wells.

Expulsive forces, whether primary or secondary, recognize no property lines—no divided ownership. They must be controlled throughout the entire reservoir for the greatest recovery. To secure the most oil for each individual, operating practices such as proper producing rates, curtailed gas production, and advantageous location of producing and injection wells must be employed. Such practices can best be achieved through a plan of unitization that gives consideration to both operating and royalty interests in the necessary readjustment of production between individual leases.

Unit operations, therefore, are designed for the further development and operation of the several properties overlying a common source of oil or gas supply as if they were one property under a single lease. Under this plan, provision is made for an equitable distribution of the production to each owner.

One procedure by which a field may be unitized is through the formation of working committees on which both operators and royalty owners are represented. The committee prepares a plan for future development and operation that will establish each owner's fair share of the future production. The division of unit interest among the various tracts of land may be established on a basis of acreage, sand volume, current production, past accumulated production, predicted future production, bottom-hole pressures, well potentials, or a combination of any two or more of these or any other factors which may be related to the producing properties. No single formula for calculation of equities will apply to all fields. One must be established for each individual field that will take into consideration the conditions which exist at the time the field is unitized, such as the type of reservoir, its controlling energy, and its stage of depletion.

Unit operations contemplate that future development and production will be carried on by one party or *Unit Operator*. The Unit Operator acts as the agent of the Operating Committee to carry out the plans established for the best interest of all parties concerned. The Operating Committee handles all affairs of the unit and is composed of one member for each operating interest. Various subcommittees may be formed to aid the Operating Committee in the management of the unit. The engineering and geological subcommittees are active in recommending proper operational procedures, and their combined skills are available to all persons with unit interest.

CHAPTER IV

FIELD EXAMPLES

Gas Injection-oil Reservoirs

The Shuler Jones sand oil reservoir in Union County, Arkansas, illustrates the way in which pressure maintenance by gas injection increases recovery. The boundaries of the reservoir and the location of production and gas-injection wells are shown in Figure 40. The injection wells are located at the top of the structure to induce a gas-cap expansion type of operation. Four years after discovery 16.7 million barrels, or approximately 17 per cent of the estimated 100 million barrels of oil-in-place, had been produced. Reservoir pressure had declined to 50 per cent of the original. The field was then unitized and gas-injection operations started. In the nine years since that time approximately 33 million barrels of the oil-in-place have been recovered, bringing the total oil recovery to 50 million barrels. Had the field continued

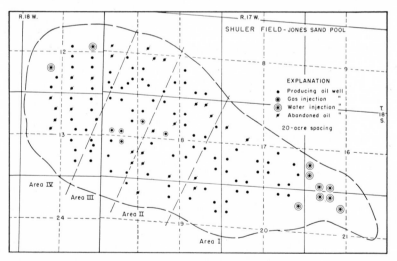

Fig. 40.—Map of Shuler field, Arkansas.

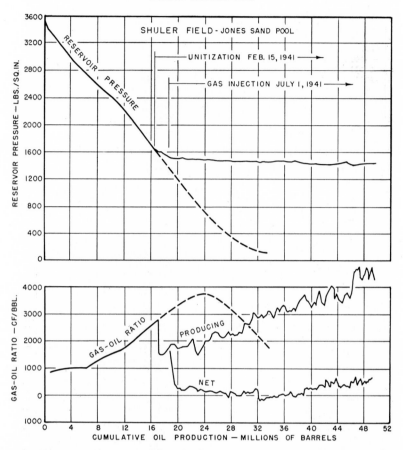

Fig. 41.—Pressure and gas-oil ratio curves before and after
unitization, Shuler field, Arkansas.

to produce under pressure-depletion operations, the ultimate recovery would have been 32 to 34 million barrels or only 32 to
34 per cent of the total. Hence about 18 million barrels or over
50 per cent more oil has already been recovered by unit operation.

The reservoir pressure and gas-oil ratio performance trends
are shown on Figure 41. The drop in the field gas-oil ratio immediately after unitization resulted from the shutdown of the high
gas-oil ratio wells and production from the low-ratio wells. This
in itself increases oil recovery because the gas in the reservoir

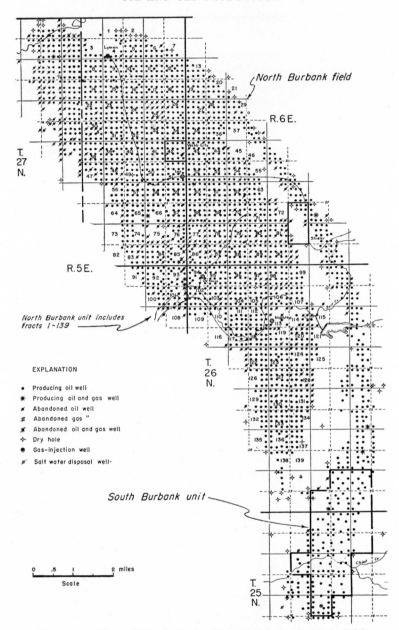

Fig. 42.—Map of North Burbank field. South Burbank field
(lower right), Oklahoma.

is then produced from those wells which can use it more efficiently. Continued selection of the wells to be produced has greatly retarded the rate of gas-oil ratio increase over the nine years of unit operations.

A comparison of the oil recovered from the North and South Burbank fields located in north central Oklahoma shows the benefits of unitization when gas-injection operations are employed in the production of oil. The pattern of development and area of the fields are shown in Figure 42. These fields produce from the Burbank sandstone and from reservoirs similar in all respects except that the thickness in the South Burbank field is fifty-three feet as compared with forty-seven feet in the North Burbank field, and the North Burbank field covers approximately ten times as

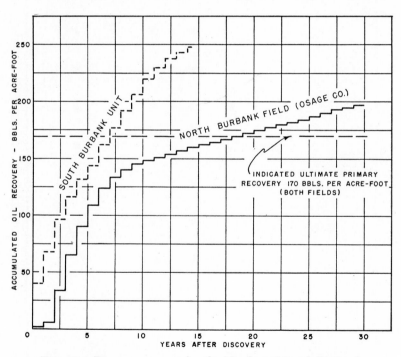

Fig. 43.—Recovery curves for the North and South Burbank fields, Oklahoma. The South Burbank field has recovered more oil for its size per acre-foot than the North Burbank field, and in one-half the time.

71

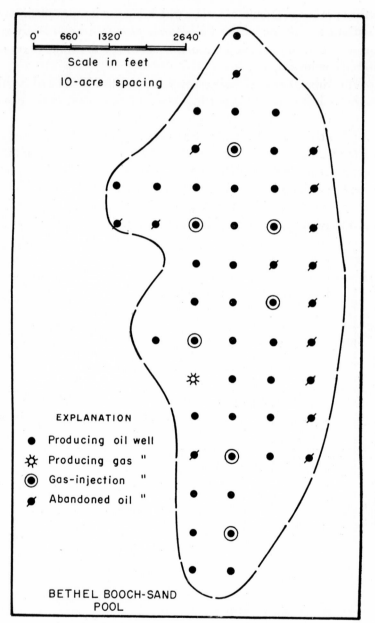

Fig. 44.—Map of Bethel field, Oklahoma.

much area as the South Burbank field. The properties of the oil produced are similar, and oil recoveries from each pool may be directly compared on an acre-foot basis to arrive at an estimate of the benefits of early unitization.

The North Burbank reservoir was discovered in 1920, and ten years later, in 1930, gas injection was commenced on a co-operative basis. The South Burbank reservoir was discovered in 1934, unitized the following year, and gas injection started immediately. North Burbank was developed on ten-acre spacing, whereas South Burbank was developed with one well to each seventeen and one-half acres. Both fields would have had a primary recovery of 170 barrels per acre-foot without unitization or gas injection. The North Burbank field has recovered 192 barrels of oil per acre-foot as a result of the co-operative gas injection commenced ten years after discovery of the field. The increase amounts to 13 per cent of the primary recovery. The South Burbank field, which was unitized and subjected to gas injection only

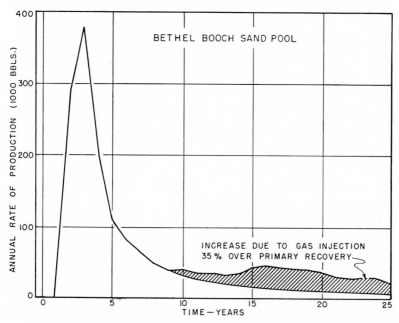

Fig. 45.—Production curve, Bethel field, Oklahoma.

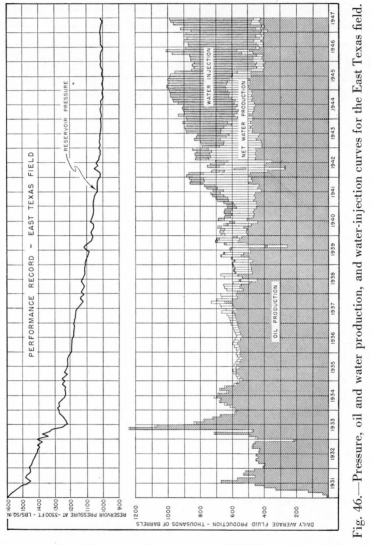

Fig. 46.—Pressure, oil and water production, and water-injection curves for the East Texas field.

one year after discovery, has recovered 248 barrels of oil to the acre-foot. This is 45 per cent more oil than would have been recovered under primary operations.

Production curves for both fields are shown in Figure 43.

The Bethel Booch sand reservoir in Seminole County, Oklahoma (Figure 44), has been operated as a gas-injection project.

74

Gas injection was started when pressures were almost depleted during the ninth year of the life of the field. Oil was produced by artificial lift, and power requirements necessitated the purchase of make-up gas. Production trends established during both primary production and gas-injection operations indicate 35 per cent more oil will be recovered (Figure 45).

In the East Texas field, water has been returned to the reservoir sand to maintain pressures and increase the ultimate oil recovery, and also as a means for disposal of the water. A natural water-drive exists, but it is not sufficiently active to maintain the reservoir pressure at the rate oil is produced. The pressure has not declined since 1942 even though the oil-production rate has been practically constant (Figure 46). The additional oil which will be recovered from this one field by returning water to the

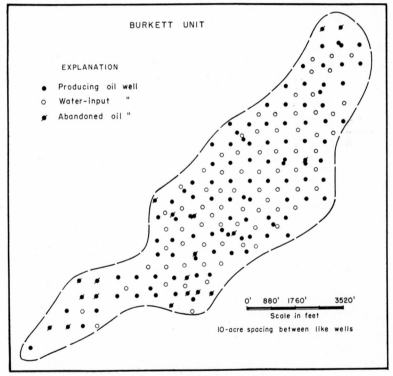

Fig. 47.—Map of Burkett field, Kansas.

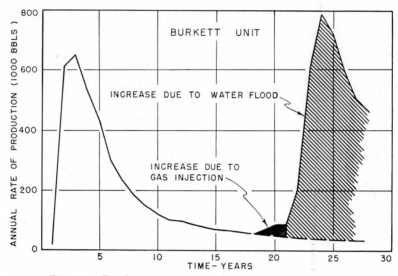

Fig. 48.—Production curve for the Burkett field, Kansas.

reservoir is estimated to be more than 600 million barrels. The increase alone is more than most fields will recover during their whole producing life.

In the Burkett field of eastern Kansas (Figure 47) additional

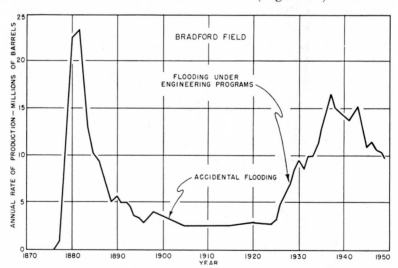

Fig. 49.—Production curve for the Bradford field, Pennsylvania.

oil has been recovered by water-flooding after depletion of its pressure by solution-gas expansion forces. The five-spot flood pattern was used. No restriction was placed on production rates during the primary life of the field. In the nineteenth and twentieth years after discovery, a gas-injection program was started and some additional oil was recovered. Gas injection was discontinued in the twenty-first year in favor of water-flooding. A rapid response to water-flooding resulted, and the oil recovered by this method will be more than that produced during the field's natural primary life (Figure 48). Not only has more oil been recovered, but it has been produced at a faster rate. In the third year after discovery of the field, the production from all wells was 651,000 barrels. In the third year after water-flooding was started, 785,000 barrels of oil were produced.

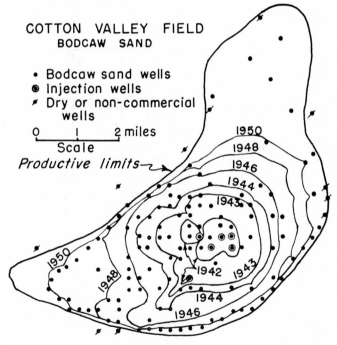

Fig. 50.—Map of the Cotton Valley field, Louisiana. The lines labeled in two-year periods show the yearly advance of the dry-gas front as it swept to the producing wells.

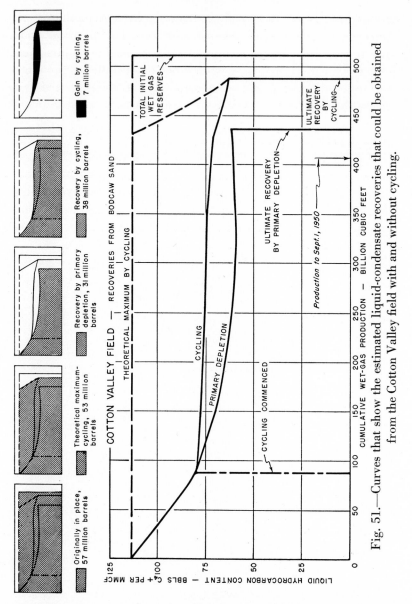

Fig. 51.—Curves that show the estimated liquid-condensate recoveries that could be obtained from the Cotton Valley field with and without cycling.

Many reservoirs have produced as much oil by water-flooding as was produced through primary pressure-depletion operations. The Bradford field in Pennsylvania has been under water-flood operation for twenty-seven years (Figure 49) and has produced during that period 264 million barrels of oil. This is 28 million barrels more than the 236 million produced during the preceding fifty years of primary life. Continued water-flood operation will add at least an additional 100 million barrels to the oil recovery.

Cycling-gas-condensate Reservoirs

The Bodcaw gas-condensate reservoir in Cotton Valley, Louisiana (Figure 50) was produced for four years prior to the time cycling operations began. During this period the reservoir pressure dropped from 4,000 psia to 3,300 psia, a rate of 175 psi per year. Retrograde condensation occurred in the reservoir, and the liquid condensate in the produced gas dropped from 115 to 82 barrels per million cubic feet, more than 8 barrels per million each year. In the nine years that the field has been operated as a unit, cycling has reduced the pressure-decline rate to 72 psi a year. The liquid condensate in the produced gas is presently 69 barrels per million cubic feet. This amounts to a yearly decline of 1.5 barrels per million cubic feet as compared with 8 barrels prior to formation of the unit, and the condensate recovery for the entire reservoir has been increased from 31 million barrels to 38 million barrels (Figure 51).

After the condensate is removed from the produced gas at the cycling plant, the dry gas is injected into centrally located wells. The wet gas is displaced toward the producing wells, and the dry-gas area gradually advances toward the edge of the reservoir (Figure 50). An efficient cycling program under unit operation could have been accomplished with only 52 of the 146 wells drilled.

The use of electrical models as a guide in the operation of cycling projects is widespread. In many ways the resistance of an electric conductor is similar to that which a permeable rock offers to the flow of fluids through it. They are so nearly alike that an electrical scale model of a reservoir can be used to predict its future performance. A scale model was assembled for the Cotton Valley field, where each electric terminal represented a

79

well. Electricity was put in at the terminals corresponding to injection wells and taken out at terminals representing the producing wells. The rate at which the current was put in and taken out is analogous to the respective volumes injected and produced for each well in the field. Based upon the scale model, a prediction was made of the area to be swept by the injected gas (Figure

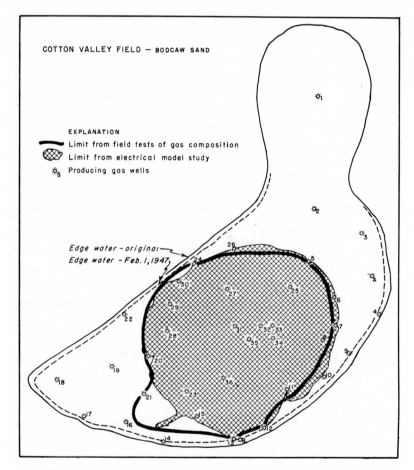

Fig. 52.—Map of Cotton Valley field. Comparison between actual area of dry-gas pattern and area which studies of electrical model indicated would be swept by dry-gas, as of 1947.

52). The wells in the Cotton Valley field have been tested periodically since cycling began in order to determine the progress of the dry-gas pattern. The area actually swept by the injected gas agrees closely with the predictions based upon the electrical scale model of the field.

CHAPTER V

MEASUREMENT IN THE PRODUCTION OF OIL AND GAS

Introduction

The development of a more or less nontechnical field of knowledge into a science proceeds so slowly that the stages in its growth are not always sharply defined to those who work with it. These changes can be seen more clearly by looking backward over the stages of development. This is particularly true in the science of oil and gas production, which is regarded by many persons to have reached maturity with the invention and application of the bottom-hole-pressure measuring tool.

The future performance of wells, tracts, and pools under specified operating conditions may be predicted by a careful analysis of a number of measurements. Forecasts of pressure changes and of the total recoverable oil and gas under different assumed practices can be made with reasonable accuracy. Changes in saturation, formation volume factors, gas-oil ratios, relative permeability, oil viscosity, well productivity, and production rates are quantitatively related to the changes in pressure and are also predictable.

Measurement in Drilling

The modern drilling rig is equipped with devices that measure the weight on the bit, the torque applied to the drill stem by the rotary table, the rate of penetration of the formation being drilled, the pressure at the wellhead on the drilling fluid, rotational speed of the drill stem, the weight of the drilling fluid, and acidity or alkalinity and viscosity of the drilling fluid. Many of these measurements are continuously recorded in modern well-logging, traveling laboratories. Some measurements must be taken only periodically. Others are shown on indicator gauges so placed that they can be continuously observed. Analysis of these measurements makes it possible to increase the efficiency of the drilling operation.

The verticality of the hole, or what is commonly thought of

Fig. 53.—Drawing of a crooked hole.

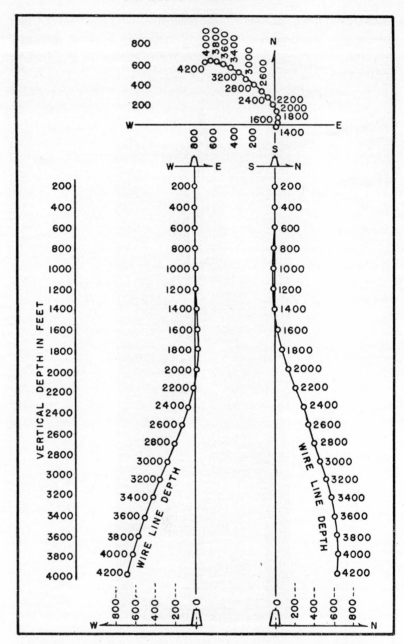

Fig. 54. Data in graph form used to make drawing in Fig. 53.

as its crookedness, is measured periodically. Usually such measurements are taken at intervals of 500 feet or more and permissible deviations seldom exceed 3 per cent (Figures 53 and 54).

Directional drilling is controlled deviation from verticality. The objective may be the bottom of another well which is out of control at the surface, sands that lie beneath lands where surface-drilling equipment is not permitted, underwater areas unsuitable for marine-derrick substructures, or a series of holes drilled from a single derrick but reaching outward in several directions.

The practice of running *electric, gamma-ray,* and *neutron logs* has become almost universal. All three of these logs help to improve the correlation of formations. They aid in finding gas, oil, or water-bearing formations in addition to providing accurate data concerning formation thickness. Electric logs (Figure 55) are run with the drilling fluid in the hole before setting pipe. Steel does not interfere with the passage of gamma and neutron rays and these logs can be obtained either before or after the pipe has been set.

Drill Stem Test

Traces of oil or gas found while drilling through a formation are tested by a method known as a *drill stem test*. The drilling fluid exerts the back pressure on the formation, but the drilling fluid must be removed in order to find out if the formation will produce oil or gas in commercial quantities. A special tool is run into the well, attached to the empty drill pipe, and placed opposite the formation to be tested. This isolates the formation from the rest of the hole, and the back pressure is removed so that any fluids present in the formation can enter the drill pipe. The rate that the oil or gas enters is measured and the formation pressure is recorded. From these data the ability of the formation to yield oil or gas is indicated.

Depth

The depth of the hole is one of the first measurements recorded at the completion of oil and gas wells. This was first done with a series of flags or strings tied to the drilling cable or sand line at regular, measured intervals. The number of such flags or strings was counted as the bailer or drilling tools were pulled from bottom.

Several types of steel line are available that read the depth directly on a counterdial (Figure 56). In deep wells these meas-

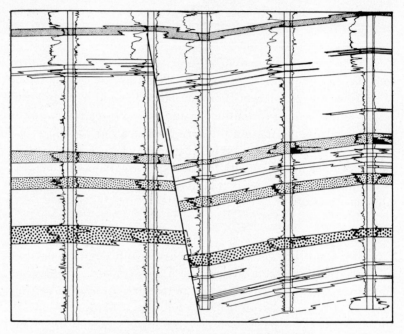

Fig. 55.—Electric-log sections of five wells in a Texas Gulf Coast field. Rock formations indicated by the logs are shown. The subsurface fault (center) was found through study of these logs.

urements are corrected for the stretch of the steel line. Depth measurements are used to determine the total depth of the hole, or the depth to fluid, lost tools, collapsed pipe, particular strata whose correlation is sought, or cement slugs whose temperature is desired, as well as to locate particular points from which controlled deviation may start.

86

Well Diameters

Various types of calipers have been developed to measure the diameter of a well bore at any depth (Figure 57). The results are recorded electrically at the surface. This information is used to calculate the volume of cement slurry or plastic that may be necessary to fill the annular space between the pipe and the walls

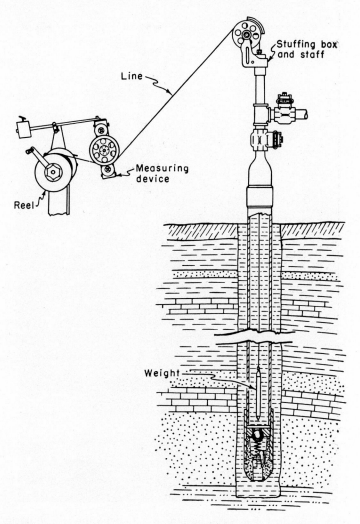

Fig. 56.—Steel line and accessories used to measure well depth.

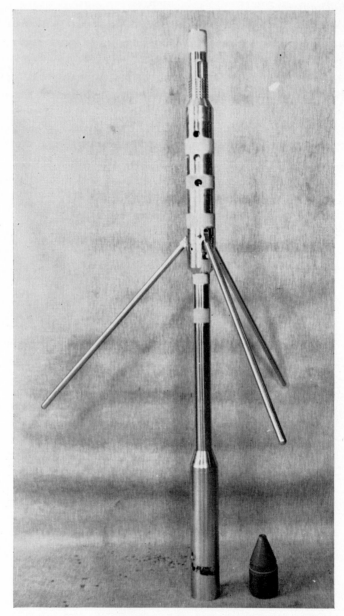

Fig. 57.—Caliper that is run into the well to determine the diameter.

of the hole to a specified or predetermined height. It is also useful in the determination of the quantity of plastic or cement needed to fill the hole when plugging back to a shallower producing formation.

Core Analyses

Various types of coring tools are used to take full-hole cores, small-diameter cores (Figure 58), and side-wall cores. Many wells are now cored all the way through the productive sand. Specimens of these cores, in addition to samples of cuttings recovered in the drilling operations, are taken to the laboratory for measurement of porosity, permeability, connate water content, and oil saturation.

Porosity is the relative volume of the pore spaces between the mineral grains compared to the total rock volume. It indicates the space available to hold oil, gas, and water. Several laboratory

Fig. 58.—Small-diameter cores of rock formations.

89

methods are used for the measurement of porosity. Although the usual range of porosities is from 15 to 20 per cent, they may be as high as 43 per cent or more in highly fractured and cavernous limestones.

Permeability is a measure of the conductivity of a rock to the movement of fluids through it. In the laboratory, permeability of dry cores is usually measured with air, gas, or water, although other liquids may be used. This measurement is described as the

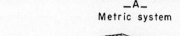

_A_
Metric system

Absolute pressure at *a* = 2 atmospheres → *a* [cube] *b* → Absolute pressure at *b* = 1 atmosphere

1 centimeter cube

If rate of flow is 1 cubic centimeter per second for a liquid with a viscosity of 1 centipoise the permeability is 1 darcy.

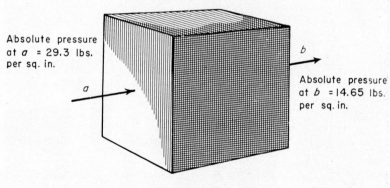

_B_
Equivalent English units

Absolute pressure at *a* = 29.3 lbs. per sq. in.

a →   *b* →

Absolute pressure at *b* = 14.65 lbs. per sq. in.

1 cubic foot

Rate of flow for same liquid as in **A** *is equal to 16.565 barrels per day. The rate is 1.1307 barrels if the difference in pressure between sides a and b is 1 pound per square inch.*

PERMEABILITY UNITS

Fig. 59.—Permeability units.

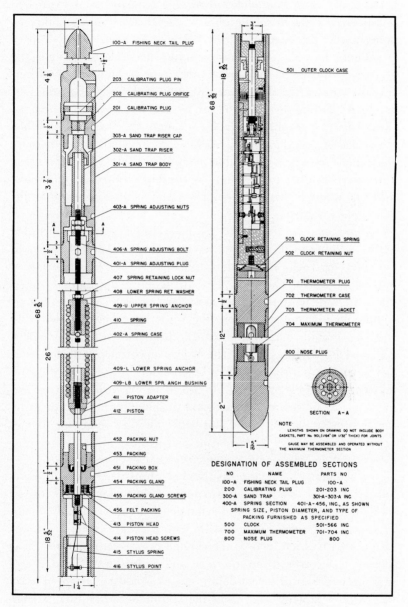

Fig. 60.—Detailed cross section of a pressure bomb.

permeability to a homogeneous fluid. Permeability is expressed in units called the *darcy* (Figure 59) or the *millidarcy* (one one-thousandth of a darcy).

Where more than one phase of fluid is flowing, such as gas and oil or gas and water, the permeability may be enormously different from that when there is a single fluid. Even though the permeability as measured in the laboratory has a definite or fixed value, that value holds only for a single fluid or phase. When a mixture of two phases is present in the flow stream, it is more convenient to express the effective permeability as a percentage of the permeability to the single phase. The term *relative permeability* is used for this purpose. The latter is always less than the homogeneous permeability.

Water and oil saturation are the relative volumes occupied by these fluids in the pore spaces between the mineral grains of the reservoir rock. These saturations can be readily determined in the laboratory. The method of coring, however, and the subsequent treatment of the cores may cause great changes in their water and oil content. Where the wells have been drilled with water-base muds, part of the natural fluid content may have been replaced by drilling fluid. The true proportions of the various fluids originally present cannot be obtained by analysis of a core that contains drilling fluid. By use of oil-base muds in coring, more nearly accurate measurement of the amount of water originally present can be made, and hence the oil content computed.

Pressure and Temperature Measurements

Of the many oil-field measurements, pressure may well be regarded as the independent variable. Other measurements are more or less related to pressure changes. Pressure is usually measured with a bottom-hole-pressure bomb (Figure 60) or gauge (Figure 61) which records the change in pressure that occurs as the bomb is lowered into the hole and withdrawn. The pressure measurements at different depths are recorded on charts (Figure 62). Under flowing conditions the bottom-hole pressure is commonly measured at several different rates of flow in order to compute a theoretical value for maximum delivery or productivity.

The bottom-hole-pressure gauges carry a special compartment for a thermometer so that both temperature and pressure can be measured. Usually the only temperature measured is the maximum which is normally at the bottom of the well. The temperature may be measured by recording devices to determine the true thermal gradient. While cement is in the chemical process of hardening, its temperature increases. A sharp change in the thermal gradient indicates the position of the top of the cement in the annular space between the casing and the wall of the hole.

Pressures at the wellhead, known as the shut-in casinghead or tubing pressures, have been measured for many years by means of a standard indicating gauge. The pressure in gas wells may be measured under flowing conditions or after the well has been shut in for some prescribed period of time, ordinarily not less than twenty-four or more than seventy-two hours. The pressure of new gas wells may rise to the maximum within a few minutes. Other wells may not reach their maximum value for several weeks. A slow rise in pressure indicates low permeability of the producing formation, while rapid rise in pressure indicates high permeability.

Static or shut-in wellhead pressures and flowing or producing

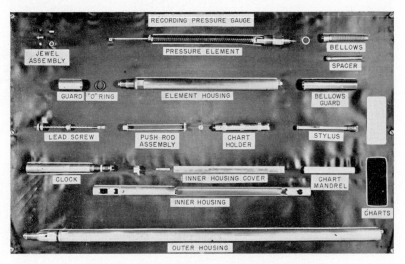

Fig. 61.—Recording pressure gauge parts.

93

pressures in oil wells are also measured. Indicating pressure gauges and recording gauges, installed on the *Christmas tree* or wellhead fittings, are used for these measurements.

The original pressure in many underground reservoirs is approximately equal to that exerted by a column of salt water equal to the depth of the reservoir, or about forty-four pounds per square inch for each one hundred feet of depth.

What is the value of pressure measurements? The decline in average pressure of the oil or gas in the formation may be a measure of the amount of depletion that has taken place at that part of the reservoir. In gas reservoirs where the pressure of the gas is the only source of energy for movement of the gas to the well

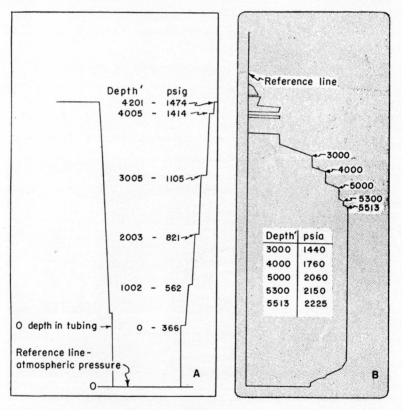

Fig. 62.—Pressure charts recorded at different depths in two wells.

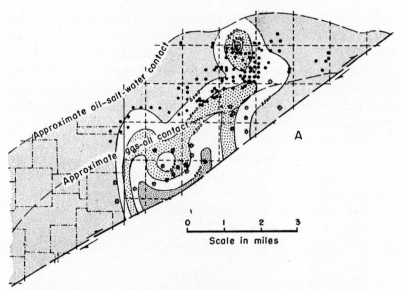

Fig. 63a.—Bottom-hole-pressure map of an oil and gas reservoir.

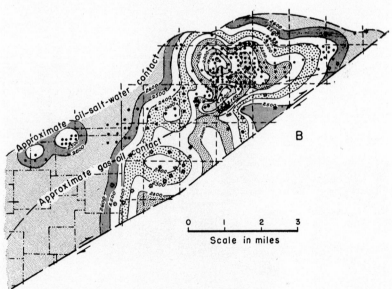

Fig. 63b.—Bottom-hole-pressure map of oil and gas reservoir
of Fig. 63a eight months later.

bore, a decline in average pressure of 10 per cent from the original pressure of the reservoir indicates that approximately 10 per cent of the recoverable gas has been withdrawn. In oil reservoirs where solution gas is the primary source of energy for movement of oil to the well bore, a specific decline in the average pressure of the entire reservoir often is an indication of the recoverable oil that may be produced during a period of similar pressure decline.

The decline in pressure of an oil field is accompanied by changes in the quantity of gas in solution, changes in the viscosity and surface tension of the oil, and changes in densities of the oil and gas as well as in their composition. These changes are closely related to changes in pressure. If the pressure is known, the other variables mentioned can be read directly from graphic data (Figure 23) or can be computed.

The weighted average reservoir pressure used in the calculation of oil and gas reserves is determined from maps on which

Fig. 64.—Mechanical separators (vertical type).

Fig. 65.—Mechanical separator (portable horizontal type).

contour lines connect points of equal pressure. These maps also depict the pressure distribution throughout the reservoir (Figures 63a and 63b).

Well Fluids

The produced fluids—oil, gas, and water—are segregated in mechanical separators (Figures 64 and 65) with the aid, at times, of chemical treatment and the application of heat.

The water is stored in evaporation pits or injected through disposal wells into non-oil-bearing sands. In some instances it is returned to the productive reservoir below the oil-water contact to aid in maintaining pressure. The gas is piped either to a gasoline plant or to a gas-transmission line or reinjected into the formation. Occasionally, but only where the gas production cannot be otherwise utilized, it is flared to the open air.

The oil is piped to storage tanks (Figure 66) to await trans-

Fig. 66.—Storage tanks (left) to which oil is piped from separators (right).

mission to pipe lines. When it is ready for sale, the depth of the oil in the storage tanks is measured together with the temperature and the gravity. After the tanks have been emptied, the depth and temperature are again measured and the volume of oil that has been sold is computed. The volume and gravity as measured are then converted to a standard volume and gravity at 60° F. upon which payment is based.

The *gravity* of the oil produced is expressed in units designated as *A.P.I. gravity*. The relation of the specific gravity to the A.P.I. gravity is as follows:

$$\text{Degrees A.P.I.} = \frac{141.5}{\text{specific gravity}} - 131.5$$

Standard practice requires that the correct value for gravity be expressed at 60° F. Various forms of hydrometers used for the measurement of the gravity read directly both the gravity and the temperature, or the gravity alone.

Viscosity is a measure of the mobility of a fluid and is usually expressed in centipoises. For example, gas flows more readily than water and water more readily than stock-tank oil. Gas, therefore, is the least viscous and oil the most viscous. Viscosities of reservoir oil range from 0.16 to 315 centipoises and gas from

Fig. 67.—Operator changing an orifice in orifice-meter installation at a gasoline-plant location.

99

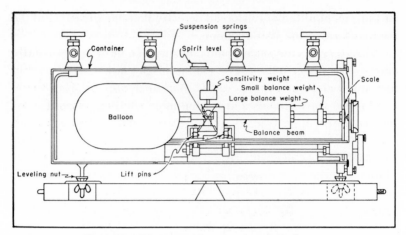

Fig. 68.—Diagram of a gas gravity balance.

0.01 to 0.09 centipoises. The more gas dissolved in the oil, therefore, the less viscous is the oil and gas mixture.

Frequently a sample of the stock-tank oil is run through a small centrifuge in order to ascertain the percentage of *water* still remaining in the oil. A reduction is made in the price of the oil for water content; if the oil carries more than 2 per cent water, it may not be accepted by the pipe line.

Several devices are in use to measure *gas*. The most common is the orifice meter (Figure 67), which is used to obtain data for computation of the volumes of gas produced for either processing or sale to pipe-line companies. The gravity of the gas is necessary

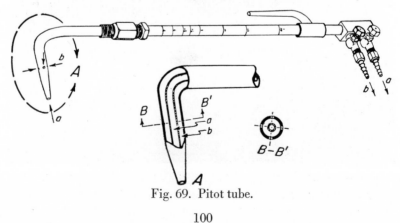

Fig. 69. Pitot tube.

100

in these computations. It is commonly measured separately by means of a gas-gravity balance (Figure 68). Either the pitot tube (Figure 69) or the orifice well tester (Figure 70) provides a fairly satisfactory method of gas measurement if the gas volumes are small.

In the measurement of gas for delivery to the major natural-gas transmission lines that comprise the connecting link between supply and market, the gas is measured almost exclusively by means of the orifice meter. The meters may be located at the lease boundary, where several wells deliver through a gathering system of lines to a single meter, and thence to the transmission line. In other instances a separate orifice meter is placed at each indi-

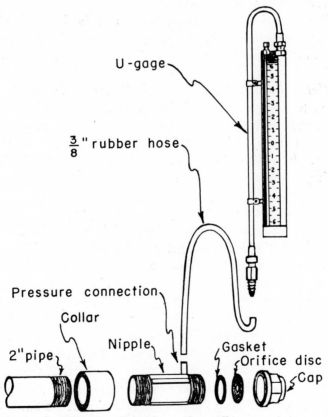

U-gage

$\frac{3}{8}$" rubber hose

Pressure connection

Collar

2" pipe

Nipple

Gasket

Orifice disc

Cap

Fig. 70.—Parts for orifice well tester.

101

vidual well. Where the gas is first passed through a compressor station or gasoline-extraction plant, the volume is also measured by orifice meters, usually placed far enough from the plant to minimize the effects of pulsations that result from compressor operations.

Gas-oil ratios are the relation between the volume of gas and the volume of oil produced. They are expressed as the number of standard cubic feet of gas produced per barrel of oil. Where all of the gas production is measured, the gas-oil ratio is calculated by dividing the gas volume by the oil volume. Portable units with measurement devices mounted on trucks are convenient for determination of gas-oil ratios (Figure 71), especially where only periodic information is desired.

Gas-oil ratios are an important factor in the mechanics of reservoir operation. They may be used to determine the efficiency of production practices and to predict future reservoir performance.

Water-oil ratios are measured periodically with sufficient frequency to provide reliable information concerning increases or decreases in the ratio. Measurements are made either by sampling the flow stream or by actual measurement of the entire well stream. Water-oil ratios are also an important factor in the mechanics of reservoir operation.

Solubility-shrinkage

The large amounts of gas dissolved in reservoir oil are responsible for the difference between the volume of oil produced in the stock tank and the volume of space that same oil occupied in the reservoir. The quantitative determination of the relative volumes is largely a laboratory problem.

Samples of the reservoir fluid are taken at the bottom of the well bore with devices similar to bottom-hole-pressure bombs and brought to the surface tightly sealed. At the time these samples are taken, additional measurements of pressure and temperature within the reservoir are made. Reservoir conditions are simulated as illustrated in Figure 22, and the behavior of the fluids in the presence of changes in pressure and temperature is determined in

102

the laboratory. A graphic plot of the laboratory data (Figure 72) is widely used in oil and gas studies.

Various terms have been applied to the volume of the reservoir oil in comparison with the volume under stock-tank conditions. The two most commonly used are the *formation-volume factor* and the *shrinkage factor*. With stock-tank oil at 60° F. taken as unity, the volume of the reservoir oil is expressed as unity plus the volume increase under reservoir conditions. Formation volumes as high as 2.25 have been encountered, but the more common factors lie between 1.15 and 1.60.

The amount of any single hydrocarbon gas that will dissolve in oil depends upon the pressure on the gas-oil mixture. But most reservoir gases are composed of a mixture of light and heavy hydrocarbons. The heavier hydrocarbons dissolve in the oil more easily than the light hydrocarbons, so that the total amount of reservoir gas that will dissolve is not strictly proportional to the

Fig. 71.—Portable equipment used to measure gas-oil ratios.

reservoir pressure. However, in many instances the amount of gas that will dissolve in the oil at pressures above 500 psia has an almost direct relationship to the pressure.

In some fields the volume of gas present in the reservoir during the geologic periods of oil formation and accumulation was

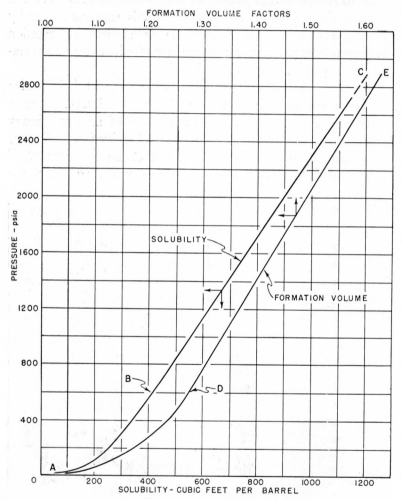

Fig. 72.—Graphs showing the changes in amount of gas in solution (ABC) and changes in volume of oil (DE) as pressures are lowered.

not sufficient to saturate the oil at the maximum pressures that were developed or that may have prevailed at the time the field was discovered. Where this condition exists, the gas in the reservoir is dissolved in the oil at the discovery date, the pressure is much greater than that necessary to produce saturation, and a gas-cap is absent. For instance, the saturation or bubble-point is below the original pressure in the East Texas reservoir. At the time of discovery, all of the hydrocarbons in the reservoir were in the liquid phase, and not until local pressures in the reservoir fell below 755 psia did the gas-cap appear along the east edge of the pool. A laboratory study of a bottom-hole sample of crude from the East Texas field shows that the volume of gas in solution (Figure 73, Curve ABCD) and the formation-volume factor (Figure 73, Curve AEFG) both increase approximately in direct proportion to the pressure until the saturation or bubble-point of 755 psia is reached (Figure 73, Points C and F). The increase in pressure above that point (Figure 73, F to G) is accompanied by a small reduction in the formation volume on account of the slight compressibility of the oil-gas solution, but all of the gas has gone into solution (Figure 73, C to D).

Solubility and formation-volume curves are used to compute the changes in volume of the reservoir fluid that result from the solution of gas therein. Calculations that involve the changes in volume of the reservoir fluids as production takes place indicate the amount of reservoir energy consumed in various parts of the reservoir.

Productivity

The productive capacity, or the ability of an *oil well* to produce expressed as barrels per hour or barrels per day, is called the well's *potential*. Fundamentally, it is a measure of the ability of the formation to deliver fluid into the well bore, but not of the amount of fluid in the reservoir.

The most common methods for its determination are these:
1. For flowing wells: The oil is produced at different rates through chokes (restricted openings) at the wellhead. The various quantities of oil produced are measured. At the

105

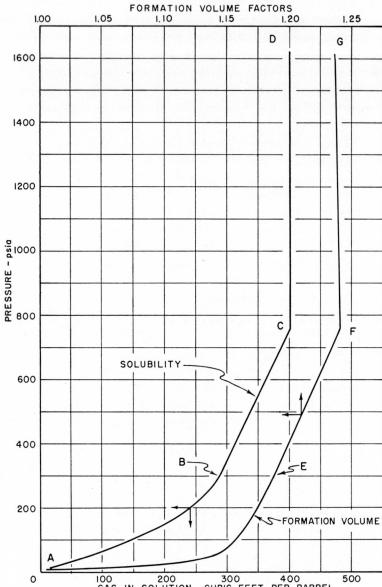

Fig. 73.—Graphs showing changes in amount of gas in solution (ABCD) and approximate changes in volume of oil (AEFG) as pressures are lowered on an oil sample from the East Texas field.

same time separate measurements of the bottom-hole pressure are made. These data are plotted on a graph (Figure 74) and the productivity index is computed. It is expressed as the rate of production per pound pressure drop at the sand face. The well's potential or capacity to produce down

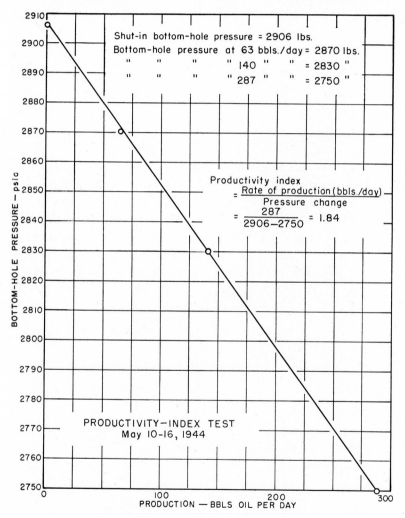

Fig. 74.—Graph of data obtained in a productivity-index test of a flowing well.

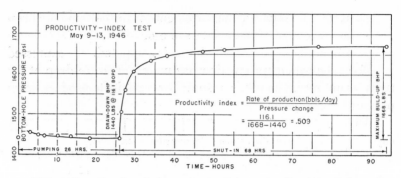

Fig. 75.—Graph of data obtained in a productivity-index
test of a pumping well.

to zero pounds pressure can then be calculated without
causing the extreme pressure drop at the sand face necessary to reduce the flowing pressure to zero.

2. For pumping wells: Measurement is made of the height
of the fluid column in the casing while the well is pumped
at different speeds. Frequent measurements of the fluid
level at one pumping speed are taken with a sonic meter
until the fluid level ceases to fall. Final readings are then
taken. The procedure is repeated until at least three sets
of readings have been taken at different pumping speeds.
These data are plotted on a graph (Figure 75) and the pro-

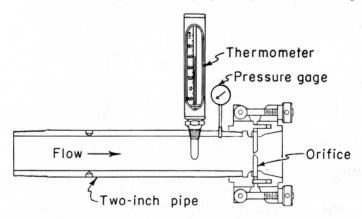

Fig. 76.—Cross section of a critical-flow prover.

ductivity index is computed. The well's potential can then be calculated without pumping the well at its maximum capacity.

Both of these methods for determining capacity or productivity of the wells avoid the waste of oil and gas without large pressure drops at the sand face.

The most common methods used to determine the productive capacity or potential of *gas wells* are these:

1. The open-flow volume is measured by means of the pitot tube and the results converted to cubic feet per day. This method is simple, but is wasteful of large volumes of gas, may damage both the formation and the well fittings, and provides little information about the well's performance under actual operating conditions.

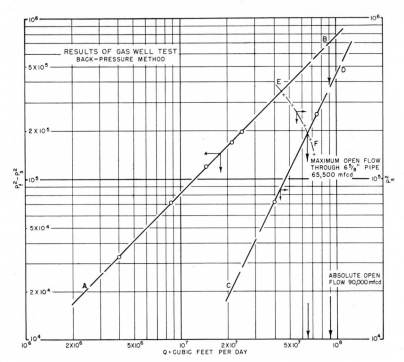

Fig. 77.—Plot based on data taken during a back-pressure test of a gas well.

109

2. In the back-pressure method, the wellhead pressures and quantities of gas produced are measured at various rates of flow. Either the critical flow prover (Figure 76) or the standard orifice meter is used to measure the gas produced. From a plot of these data (Figure 77) the amount of gas the well would be able to deliver against an assumed zero pressure at the wellhead or sand face or at various pipeline pressures may be computed. The back-pressure method makes it possible to determine the capacity of a gas well without waste of gas. It also eliminates the hazards of damage to the formation and well equipment.

Actually, it is impossible to reduce bottom-hole pressures to zero pounds per square inch, and the productivities thus determined must be regarded as theoretical quantities.

Note: The conditions for the measurement of a *standard cubic foot of gas* are almost everywhere placed at an absolute pressure of 14.65 pounds per square inch (psia) and a temperature of 60° F.

CHAPTER VI

REGULATORY PRACTICES
AFFECTING OIL RECOVERY

Before the mechanics of reservoir behavior were understood, wide-open flow production was almost universal. Reservoirs were drilled with dense spacing patterns. Many of the wells were unnecessary and served only as a means for one operator to drain oil from under his neighbor's land. Gas produced with the oil was conceived to be detrimental—a necessary evil that had to be removed before the oil could be recovered from the reservoir. As a result of this misconception, tremendous quantities of gas were wasted—gas that could have been used as an expulsive force in the production of additional oil. The wide-open flow rates caused inefficient water encroachment into the oil zone, trapping and making unrecoverable large volumes of oil. In some fields oil was produced too fast for the transportation facilities to handle all of it. Tanks overflowed and large quantities of oil were lost by evaporation, weathering, and fire. Co-operative action to conserve the supply of oil and gas, which is so necessary in our national economy, became imperative.

The problems involved in the production of oil and gas are numerous and vary widely among reservoirs. Conservation can be most effectively administered only by the individual states. In 1935 the Interstate Compact to Conserve Oil and Gas was formed to study and report on all phases of oil and gas production, primarily for the benefit of the oil and gas-producing states. It was designed to serve as a medium for educating the entire industry, the state regulatory bodies, federal officials, and the public on current problems in conservation. The world's foremost petroleum authorities regularly report and contribute to the Compact Commission on the latest scientific developments in oil and gas production. At its regular meetings the current and common problems of the regulatory bodies of the oil-producing states are discussed, as well as suggestions by the public, Congressional committees, and the industry. One purpose of the Compact Commission is to make inquiry and determine from time to time what new methods, practices, circumstances, and conditions may be pertinent to conservation and the prevention of physical waste of oil and gas. Its findings and recommendations are reported to the several states for adoption or rejection, as they see fit. As an outgrowth of the educational work carried on by the Compact, the states and the entire nation are assured a continued and abundant supply of the oil and gas fuels vital to our national life.

The compacting states have made great progress in the conservation of oil and gas. They are constantly making improvements in the application of conservation principles. Millions of barrels of oil which otherwise would not have been recovered have already been made available by the application of conservation principles. State controls which have remedied many of the evils of the wide-open flow era include:

1. Restriction of oil-production rates in water-drive reservoirs to near the rate at which the water encroaches in order to utilize the energy available from the movement of the water in the recovery of more oil.

2. Restriction of the rate of oil production from fields in which wells are producing with high gas-oil ratios, to prevent the waste of gas.

3. Restriction of oil production in reservoirs with gas-caps to the rate at which the gas-cap encroaches on the oil zone. In many instances the control of production from reservoirs with gas-caps has permitted the conversion of the recovery mechanism from an inefficient solution-gas expansion drive to the more efficient water-drive, or gas-cap expansion type.

4. Restrictions on producing gas-oil ratios and water-oil ratios to prevent excessive waste of the gas and water energy by the inefficient high gas-oil and water-oil ratio wells and

to prevent water-coning and by-passing of oil in water-drive reservoirs.

5. Restriction of the volume of fluid withdrawals by wells producing from gas, oil, and water zones within the same reservoir, to prevent both the migration of oil into the dry-gas zone and the waste of water energy.

6. Control of drilling and completion practices to prevent loss of oil and gas through blowouts and to insure that the section exposed to the well bore connects with the more efficient productive zones of the reservoir.

7. In addition to these restrictions, the industry is required to protect the fresh water supplies, whether surface or subsurface, from pollution.

An analysis of the behavior of oil and gas reservoirs leads to the general conclusions that:

1. the rate of fluid production is an important factor affecting recovery of oil and gas;

2. the control of the rate involves an equitable allocation of the restricted production;

3. production from that part of the reservoir which utilizes the available energy most efficiently is the best type of conservation practice;

4. an adequate number of wells must be drilled to produce the reservoir at an efficient rate—more than this number of wells constitutes excessive drilling and actual waste;

5. most reservoirs need a supplement to the natural energy in the form of gas or water injection, or both;

6. each reservoir has separate and distinct characteristics and the proper mechanics of reservoir operation must be determined for each;

7. nature formed each oil and gas reservoir as a unit, a single common source of supply;

8. maximum recoveries are possible only when a reservoir is operated as a unit without respect to surface boundaries and fences, and a fair and equitable division of the production from the entire reservoir can be made.

The Interstate Oil Compact recommends that all who are interested in conservation and wish to secure the maximum amount of oil and gas to maintain our present economic system give careful consideration to the conclusions drawn from the present knowledge of the behavior of oil and gas reservoirs. Only by the co-operative action of everyone concerned can this goal be attained.

MAJOR TYPES OF RESERVOIR TRAPS

Seven major types of reservoir traps are recognized:

I. Anticlines and Domes. This group includes the various types of upfolds regardless of their origin. They are common in most of the regions where commercial petroleum deposits are found.

Anticlines are elongated upfolds with one or more structural highs. Most anticlines are produced by compression of strata. Some are the simple type (Figures 6, 78, and 79). Some are re-folded (Figure 80). Other types of anticlines are reflected buried ridges (Figure 81) and buried elongate reef masses (Figure 11).

Domes, which are rounded or elliptical in ground plan, may also be produced by the compression of strata. Other types of domes are reflected buried hills (Figure 81), buried reef masses (Figure 11), salt domes with rudely cylindrical salt intrusions (Figure 82), and non-piercement salt domes which are produced by local thickening of salt beds (Figure 19).

II. Permeability Traps. *Differential porosity and permeability traps* are formed by loss in porosity and permeability

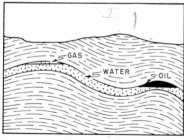

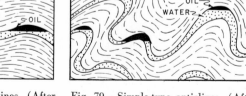

Fig. 78.—Simple-type anticlines. (After LeRoy)

Fig. 79.—Simple-type anticlines. (After LeRoy)

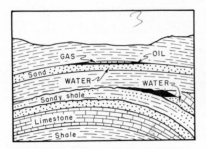

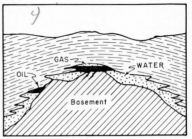

Fig. 80.—Refolded anticline. (Modified after LeRoy)

Fig. 81.—Traps in rocks that flank and overlie buried ridge. (Modified after LeRoy)

updip in the reservoir rock. The lower boundary is fixed by edge water and locally by bottom water. Lateral gradation of sandstones into shales or other impervious rocks (facies changes) or increase in cementing material decreases the porosity and permeability and may thus fix the upper boundary (Figures 8, 83, and 84). Lateral gradation commonly occurs in beds that originate under conditions of marginal marine sedimentation. In limestones and dolomites such traps result from (1) textural changes from the granular, oolitic, reef, or fragmental types to more dense carbonate-rock updip (Figures 16); (2) discontinuous porous zones caused by solution action (Figure 12); (3) gradation updip into impermeable rocks such as anhydrite and shale; and (4) secondary cementation of porous-zones updip by calcite, gypsum, or anhydrite.

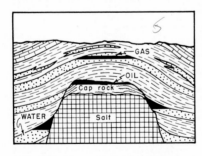

Fig. 82.—Reservoirs on a salt dome.

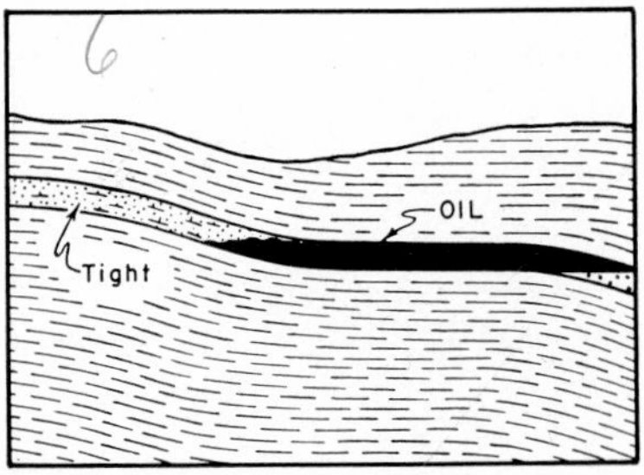

Fig. 83.—Loss in porosity and permeability in tight sand forms reservoir's upper boundary. (After LeRoy)

116

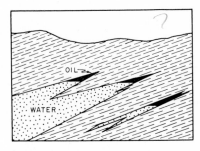

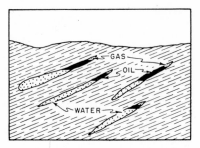

Fig. 84.—Porous sandstone reservoir grading into shale updip. (After LeRoy)

Fig. 85.—Interbedded sandstone lenses surrounded by impervious shale. (After LeRoy)

Lenticular reservoirs are limited in all directions by strata of low permeability. They occur as interbedded lenses, streaks (Figures 85, 86, and 87), or other bodies of porous and permeable rock. Many lenticular reservoirs are almost completely saturated with oil or gas. They may contain a little residual connate water and insignificant amounts of bottom water or edge water in low parts of the sand bodies. Most of them are in areas of slight structural relief and represent such features as off-shore bars, tidal channel fills, and stream channel fills. The reservoir rock grades laterally and vertically into shales or tight sands that fix the actual reservoir boundaries. The shoestring sands of the Mid-Continent region are notable examples.

Asphaltic seals may form permeability traps in reservoir rocks that are open to the surface. Seepage and deterioration of petroleum at the surface fixes the upper boundary of the reservoir

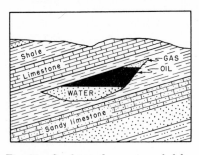

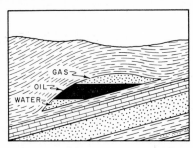

Fig. 86.—Sandstone lens surrounded by shale.

Fig. 87.—Sandstone lens surrounded by shale.

117

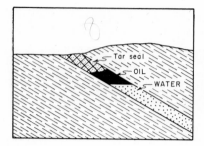

Fig. 88.—Asphaltic or tar-seal reservoir. (After LeRoy)

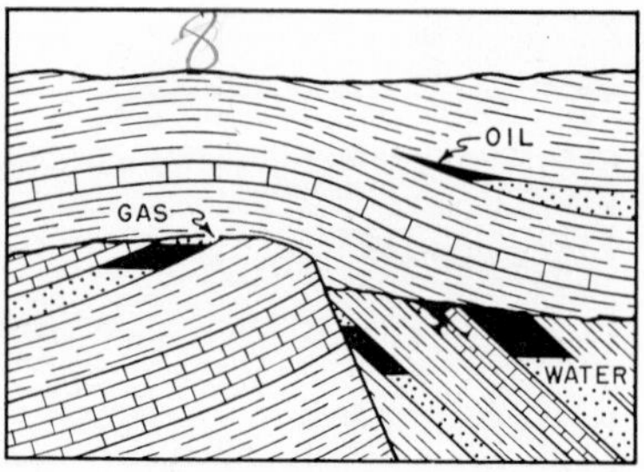

Fig. 89.—Reservoirs in truncated beds with wedge above truncated zone. (After LeRoy)

(Figure 88). Accumulations of this nature are found principally downdip from outcrops of inclined beds on the flanks of anticlines or on eroded monoclines.

III. TRUNCATION AND OVERLAP TRAPS. *Truncations* are the top ends of reservoir horizons which have been cut off by erosion and subsequently sealed by impervious beds (Figures 89 and 90). The East Texas field is a truncation on the west flank of the large Sabine uplift (Figure 91).

Overlaps are found at the base of marine deposits lying on older sedimentary deposits or basement complexes (Figure 92). The lower producing zone of the Playa del Rey structure in California is a basal conglomerate which wedges out and is overlapped on the core of the uplift.

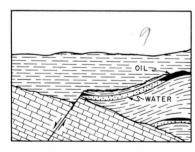

Fig. 90.—Reservoirs formed by truncation and fault. (After LeRoy)

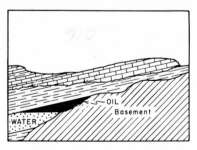

Fig. 92.—Overlap on beds that flank basement-rock mass. (After LeRoy)

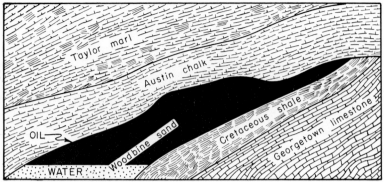

Fig. 91.—East-west cross section of East Texas reservoir.

IV. FAULT TRAPS. In this type of trap the reservoir has slipped or been displaced against an impervious rock updip. Faults occurring alone, as nearly parallel or as intersecting series, may form traps in tilted strata, particularly when impervious rocks are faulted against reservoir horizons (Figures 93 and 94) or when the faults are sealed by clay or by mineral matter deposited by circulating ground water.

Simple traps such as anticlines and domes may be broken up into several isolated traps as a result of faulting (Figures 95, 96, and 97). However, the typical fault traps, such as the Luling field, Texas, are developed on monoclinal dips where strike faults or intersecting faults have formed barriers to migration of the hydrocarbons (Figures 98 and 5).

V. PIERCEMENT TRAPS. The intrusion of molten igneous ma-

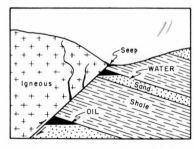

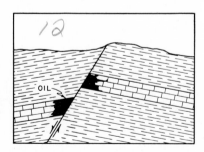

Fig. 93.—Fault traps. (After LeRoy)   Fig. 94.—Fault traps. (After LeRoy)

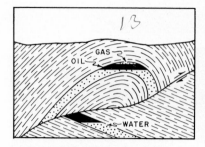

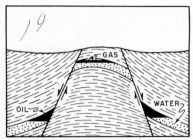

Fig. 95.—Anticline broken up into traps by fault. (After LeRoy)

Fig. 96.—Dome broken up into three traps by two faults. (Modified after LeRoy)

terial or rock salt into sedimentary rocks may seal tilted reservoir horizons and thus form possible traps for oil and gas.

In some places rock salt has intruded along the axial planes of anticlines. In other places, cylindrical plugs of rock salt, seldom more than two miles in diameter, arch the overlying strata to form salt domes. Traps of the piercement type may also be developed on the flanks of such structures (Figure 82). Intrusive bodies of igneous rocks have produced traps containing small reservoirs of oil at a few localities (Figures 99 and 100).

VI. TRAPS IN FRACTURED AND FISSURED ROCKS. Fracture zones occur in hard sandstones, limestones, cherts, and well-compacted shales. The fractures may be nearly parallel, linear, or irregular. The irregular fracture zones often follow zones of brittle rocks. In limestones and dolomites, solution action of

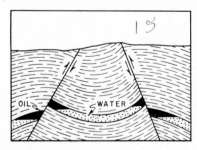

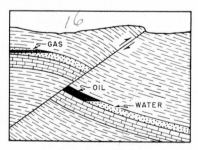

Fig. 97.—Traps in faulted syncline. (After LeRoy)

Fig. 98.—Traps on faulted monocline. (Modified after LeRoy)

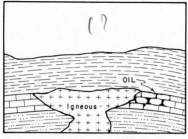

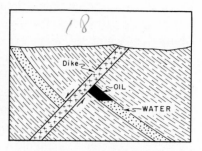

Fig. 99.—Reservoir formed by igneous intrusion. (After LeRoy)

Fig. 100.—Reservoir formed by igneous intrusion (dike). (After LeRoy)

ground water may enlarge the original fractures and fissures. The North fields of the Tampico region of Mexico, on a large regional uplift, produce from faulted and fractured limestones. Most of the oil that is produced comes from the fissures in the limestone. Very little comes from the massive, less disturbed carbonate rocks (Figure 12).

In the Florence oil field of Colorado, oil occurs in nearly vertical fissures (Figure 13). These are presumably tension cracks in the thick Pierre shale of Upper Cretaceous age along a belt where a distinct change in the rate of monoclinal dip takes place. The most important traps of the Santa Maria fields of California are fractured cherts and brittle shales of the Monterey (Miocene) formation on a monoclinal structure.

VII. COMBINATION OR COMPLEX TRAPS. Oil and gas traps

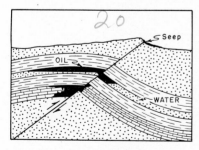

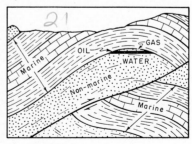

Fig. 101.—Faulted anticline reservoir. (After LeRoy)

Fig. 102.—Anticline complicated by faulting. (After LeRoy)

121

are usually more complex than the above classifications might imply, since all types of traps are subject to modifying influences. Many domes and anticlines are complicated by faulting (Figures 101 and 102), by facies changes (Figure 14), or by unconformity and facies changes (Figure 15). One or more reservoir horizons may fail to extend over the entire structure because of pinch-outs (Figure 9) or lateral gradation effects (Figure 16). The reservoir horizon may become tight high on the structure because of increases in shale content or in the amount of cementing material (Figure 18). Traps may occur in the buried ridge as well as in the overlying strata (Figure 9).

INDEX

Absolute pressure: 28 ff.
Accumulation and origin of hydrocarbons: 15–16
Age of the earth: 3
Agua Dulce, Texas: 55
Anhydrite rocks: 14
Anticlines and domes: 10, 115
Asphalt (solid hydrocarbon): 26
Asphaltic-base oil: 24, 26

Bacterial action: 15
Bedding planes: 16
Bed-key: 19
Bethel Booch sand, Oklahoma, map of: 72
Big Lake, Texas: 55
Bitumen: 26
Bottom-hole pressure: 92 ff.
Bottom-hole pressure bomb: 91, 93, 94
Bradford, Pennsylvania: 76 ff.
Bubble-point: 29, 32, 105 *see also* saturation point
Burbank field, Oklahoma: 70–71
Burkett, Kansas, map of: 75
Butane: 25 ff.
By-passing: 46

Cap, gas: *see* gas-cap
Capacities, cycling plant: 61
Capacity measurement: 105
Capacity, open-flow (gas wells): 64, 109, 110
Carbonate rocks: 13
Carbon dioxide: 24, 27, 29
Channels, pore: 24
Christmas tree: 94
Closure, structural: 17
Cloud point, oil: 26
Conglomerates: 12
Combination reservoir traps: 122
Committees, operating: 67
Complex reservoir traps: 122
Composition of natural gas: 27–28
Compressibility: 24, 32, 33, 34, 37, 38;

of reservoir gases and liquids, 32 ff.; of reservoir water, 24, 37, 38; of oil, 105
Condensate, gas: *see* gas-condensate mixtures
Condensate sampling: 57, 58
Condemnation: 33, 34
Condensation, retrograde: 56; sampling procedures, 57, 58; characteristics, 59; gas-liquid ratios, 59; maximum recovery, 59; methods of liquid extraction, 60; typical results, 60, 62; gas sales, 64
Coning, water: 46
Connate water: 22, 23, 52
Contact between fluids: 22, 23; gas-oil, 22, 41, 51; oil-water, 22, 41, 45, 49
Contour interval: 20
Contour map, structure of: 19
Controls, state: 112, 113
Core analyses: 89; connate water, 22, 23; porosity, 89; permeability, 90, 92; oil saturation, 92; relative permeability, 92; water saturation, 92
Cotton Valley, Louisiana: 55, 78, 79; map of field, 77, 80
Crude oil: 24, 26; *see also* petroleum
Crude-oil mixtures at elevated pressures: 29 ff.
Cubic foot, standard: 110
Cycling: 61, 62; gas-liquid ratios, 59; plant capacities, 61; pressure maintenance, 61; not applicable, 61; disposition of residue gas, 63; necessity for unitization, 63; gas sales, 64; need for well control, 64; production rates, 64; electrical models, 78, 80, 81; Cotton Valley, Louisiana, 79

Darcy: 90, 92
Decline in pressure: 39, 56, 94, 96
Density: reservoir liquid, 32, 33, 34; well fluids, 33, 34
Depth measurement: 85, 86
Dew point: 33
Directional drilling: 82 ff.

123

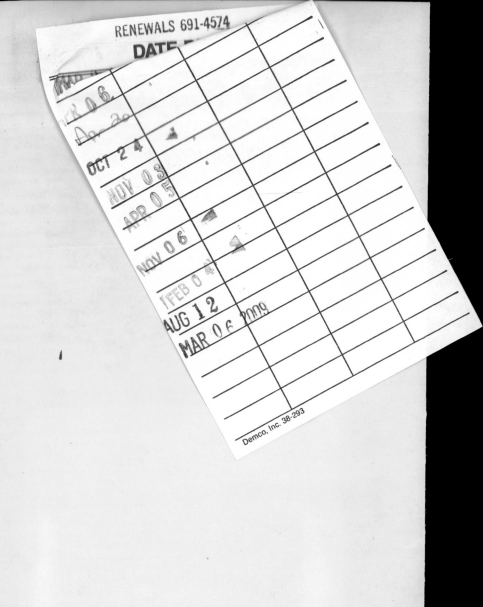